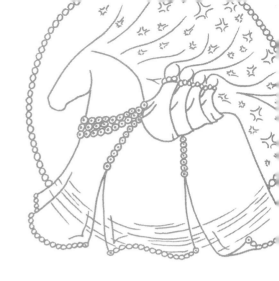

Horse Mandalas/ Mandala Horses

COLORING and DESIGN BOOK

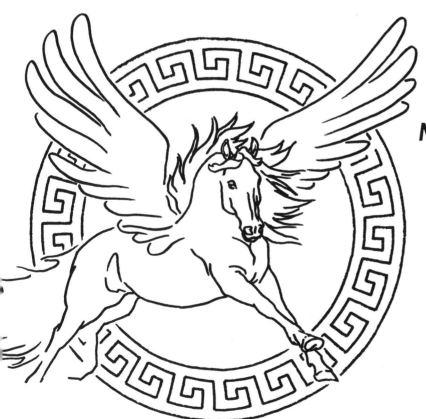

Miriam Nieuwe Weme

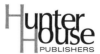

Hunter House
PUBLISHERS

Dutch edition © 2012 by Miriam Nieuwe Weme
Published by Uitgeverij Juwelenschip bv, Cothen
Original title: *Mandala Paarden * Horses * Pferde*
U.S. edition © 2012 by Hunter House Inc., Publishers

Hunter House Inc., Publishers
PO Box 2914
Alameda CA 94501-0914

Ordering
Trade bookstores in the U.S. and Canada please contact:

Publishers Group West
1700 Fourth Street, Berkeley CA 94710
Phone: (800) 788-3123   Fax: (800) 351-5073

For bulk orders please contact:

Special Sales
Hunter House Inc., PO Box 2914, Alameda CA 94501-0914
Phone: (510) 899-5041   Fax: (510) 865-4295
E-mail: sales@hunterhouse.com

Individuals can order our books by calling **(800) 266-5592**
or from our website at **www.hunterhouse.com**

Project Credits
Cover Design: Jinni Fontana   Rights Coordinator: Candace Groskreutz
Book Production: John McKercher   Customer Service Manager: Christina Sverdrup
Copy Editor: Heather Wilcox   Order Fulfillment: Washul Lakdhon
Managing Editor: Alexandra Mummery   Administrator: Theresa Nelson
Acquisitions Assistant: Elana Fiske   Computer Support: Peter Eichelberger
Special Sales Manager: Judy Hardin   Publisher: Kiran S. Rana

Printed and bound by Sheridan Books, Ann Arbor, Michigan
Manufactured in the United States of America

9 8 7 6 5 4 3 2 1   First Edition   12 13 14 15 16

Author's Note

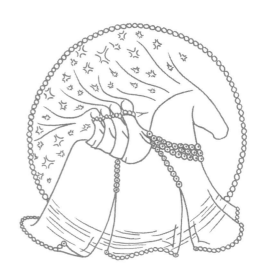

Inspiration

Horses are inspiration on four legs. If you have ever seen a horse galloping toward freedom with his head held high and his nostrils flaring wide, you know that you will never forget that image.

When I was at a dark time in my life, two special women advised me to start coloring mandalas. Working with mandalas is not just inspirational but also comforting and calming. Joyce gave me a highly detailed drawing in the shape of a rose. When I had finished coloring the final petal, I knew one thing for certain: Nothing is more frustrating than coloring a mandala. I was just too much of a perfectionist and overly focused on details, so Monique gave me three simpler, more-abstract mandalas. I tried to enjoy coloring them but thought the experience was such a shame, because I found the mandala's lines alone much more interesting.

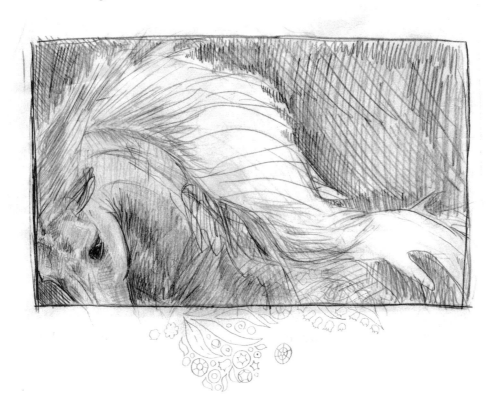

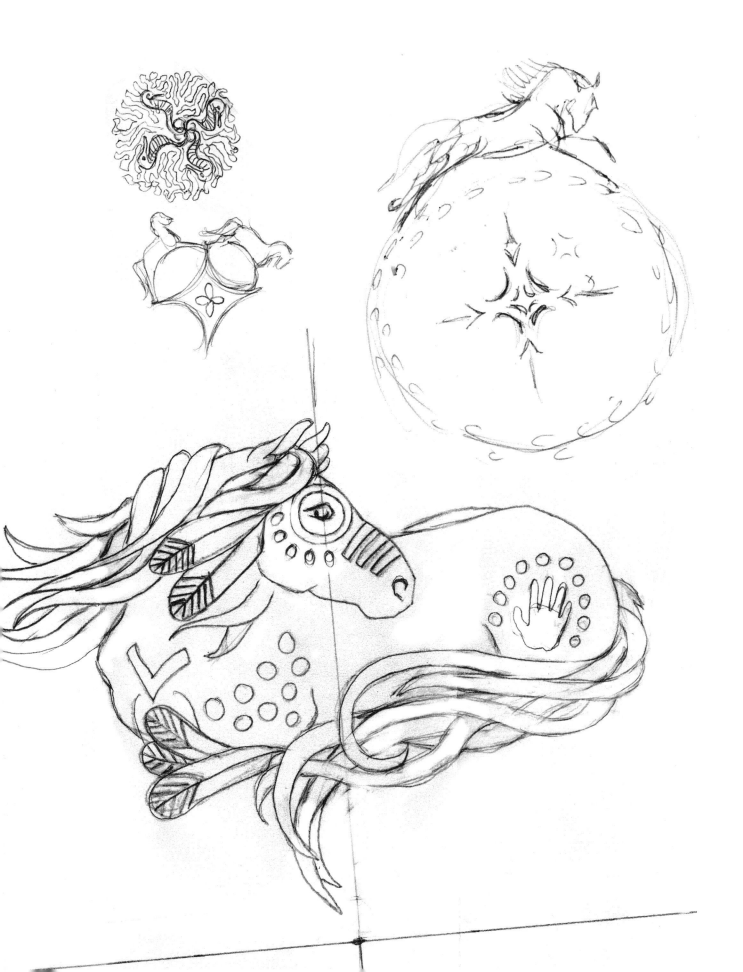

When I had finished the mandalas, the white areas were still white, but I had traced all the lines in a new color and had expanded and reshaped them. That was when Monique asked me the momentous question (for this book): "If the coloring is not working for you, and working with the lines relaxes you, why don't you design a mandala yourself? It might even inspire you to start coloring them, too."

At that moment, the horses galloping inside my head got a whiff of freedom, running free in a flood of horse-themed mandalas. I found inspiration everywhere—stained-glass windows, classical riding, mythology, tattoos, fortune dragons, IKEA, the paintings of Gustav Klimt—but above all, from the horses themselves.

I have now designed about fifty horse mandalas. Even though I have never colored one, playing with the lines and creating horses and circles is one of the most inspiring and calming activities I know. The best part, however, is realizing that others will add the colors to the mandalas that I could not. I am very curious about what you will do with these drawings, and I hope you will have as much fun coloring them as I had designing them!

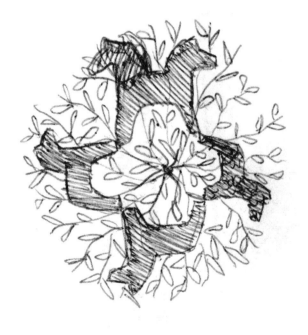

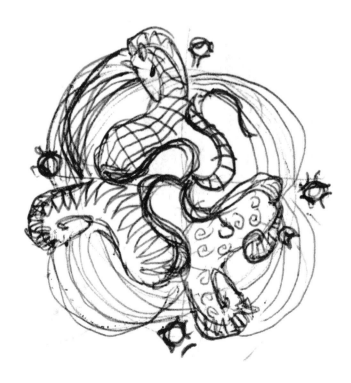

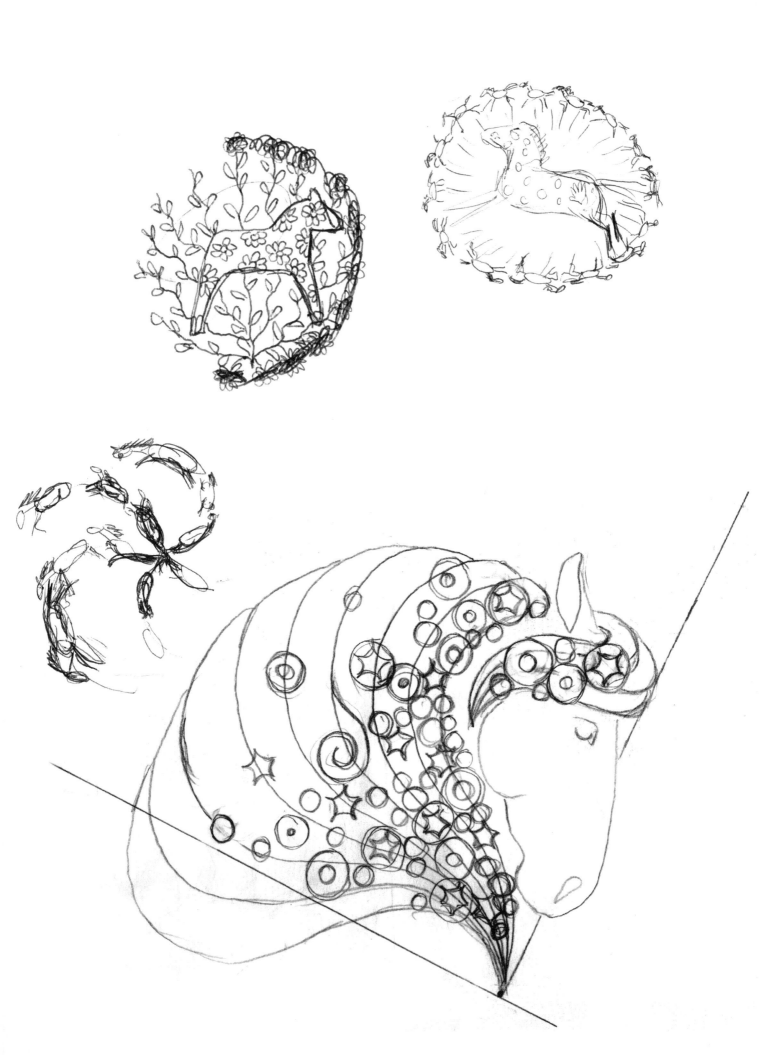

Mirrors of the Soul

I like horses best *au naturel*, without a bridle or head collar, so I depict them this way in the mandalas. Some of the horses do not have their eyes filled in yet. The eyes are also known as the mirrors of the soul, and in many cases I did not want to determine their expressions just yet. You can add their expressions yourself, if you wish, as you would add extra tack: Look at the other mandalas to see the different expressions in the horses' eyes and decide what you want your horse to express. A stylized horse's eye is not so hard to draw. Often, it is made up of no more than two lines that along with the edge of the eye create a triangle, yet you can recognize an eye in the shape. Follow where your imagination leads you and make your mandalas as personal as you want!

Coloring the Mandalas

The most important feature of a traditional mandala is its rotational symmetry. If you cut a pizza slice from the figure, you will notice that the image on that slice is repeated throughout the entire mandala. The symmetry and repetition have a calming and meditative effect, so mandalas are often colored in as symmetrically as possible. However, if the same horse is featured in a mandala eight times, that does not all eight horses have to be colored the same way. You can choose alternating colors to maintain the symmetry, but nobody will scold you for giving the horses different colors, either. Be aware of tradition, but understand that your mandala belongs to you first and foremost, so it is up to you to decide how to color it.

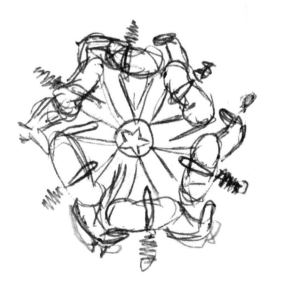

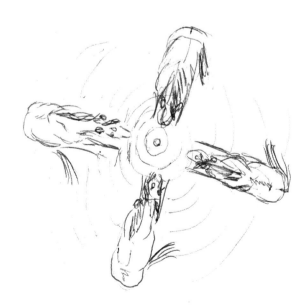

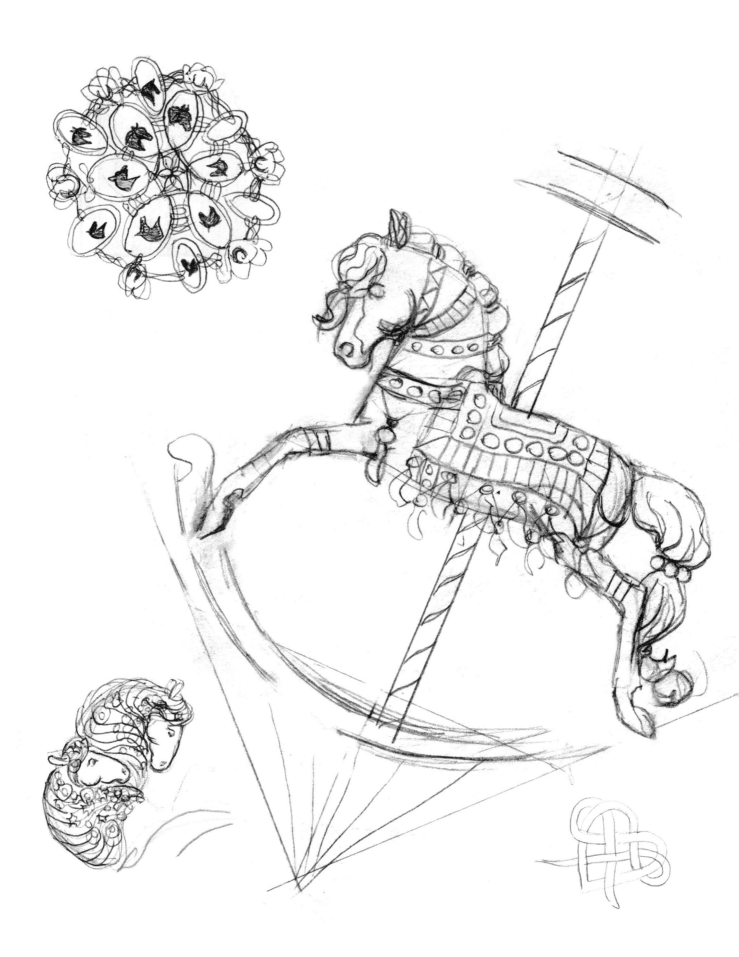

Tips

You can use a crayon or marker to color the mandalas, but you can also use Ecoline or other types of paint. Here are a few tips to get you started:

- If you want to add a detail to the drawing, such as an eye or head collar, roughly sketch the design using a pencil before tracing the lines with a black pen. You can then erase the pencil lines to make your additions indistinguishable from the lines of the original drawing.

- Put a sheet of paper underneath the mandala you want to color to prevent stains or scratches from appearing on the drawing underneath.

- The great advantage of watercolor and Ecoline paints is that they are transparent, so the black lines underneath stay visible. If you use an opaque paint, such as acrylic, stay inside the lines when coloring if you want to be able to see them.

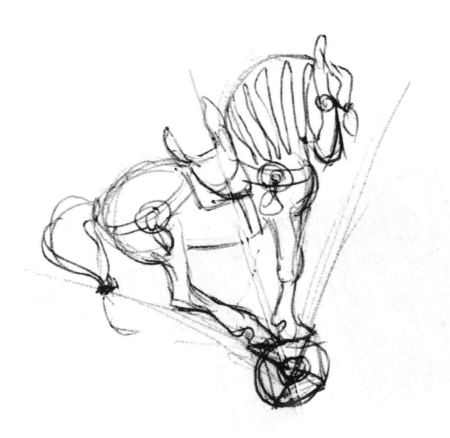

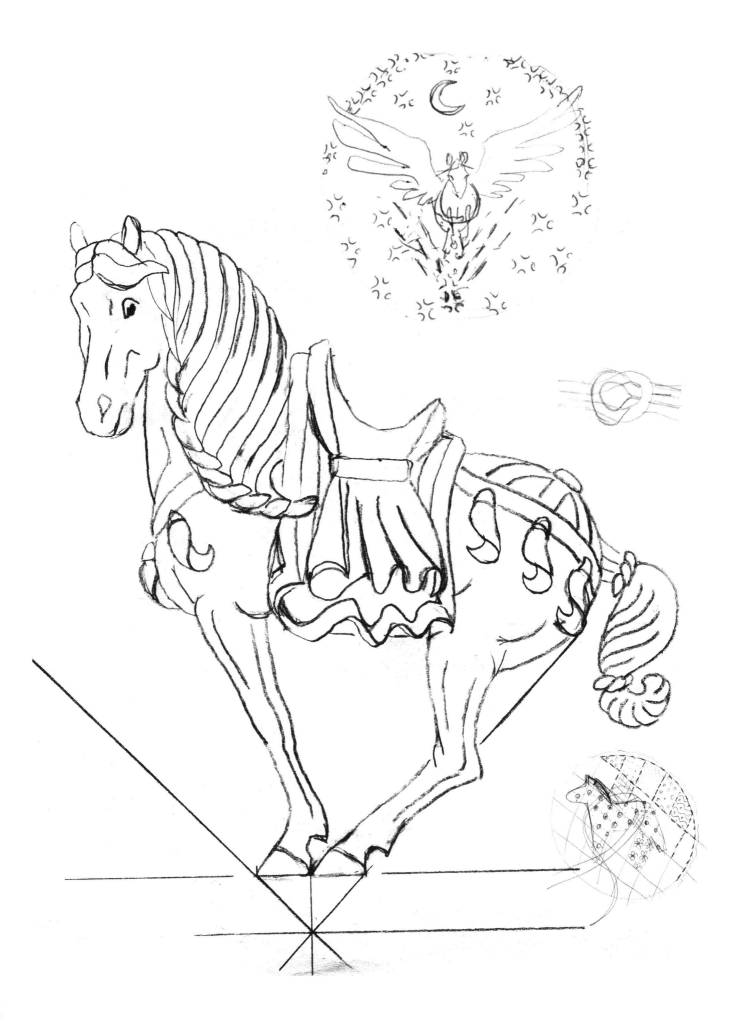

- Paper tends to wrinkle when it gets wet. Place the mandala between two sheets of blotting paper when it is still wet, and set it under a thick book or another heavy object and leave it to dry for a couple of hours. This will prevent the mandala from being wrinkled when it has dried.

- Mandalas can be shared: Surprise other people with a small, colored mandala on a card!

Miriam Nieuwe Weme

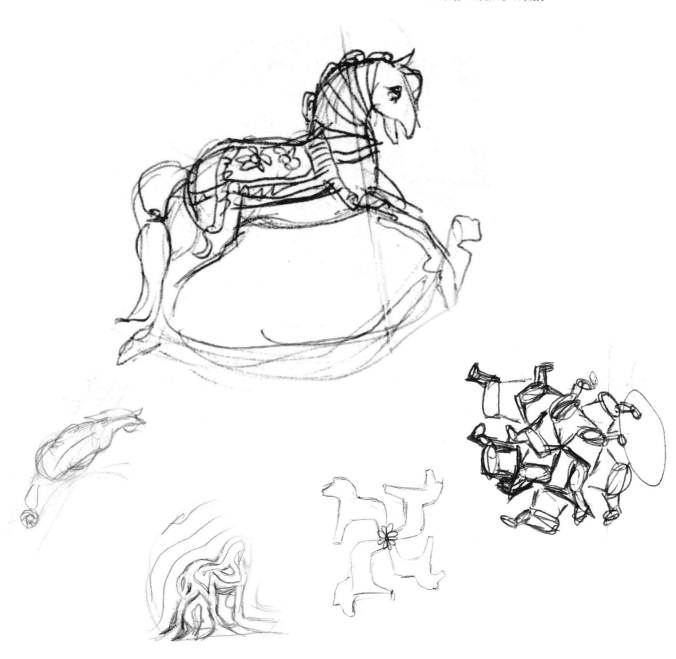

The Mandalas

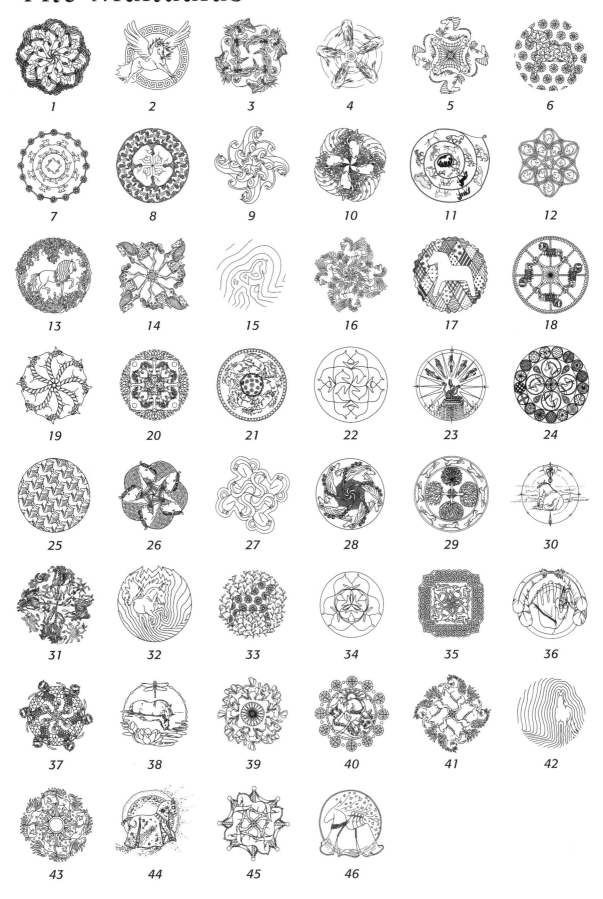

1

2

3

4

5

6

7

8

9

10

11

12

13

14

15

16

17

18

19

20

21

22

23

24

25

26

27

28

29

30

31

32

33

34

35

36

37

38

39

40

41

42

43

44

45

46

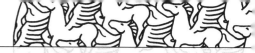

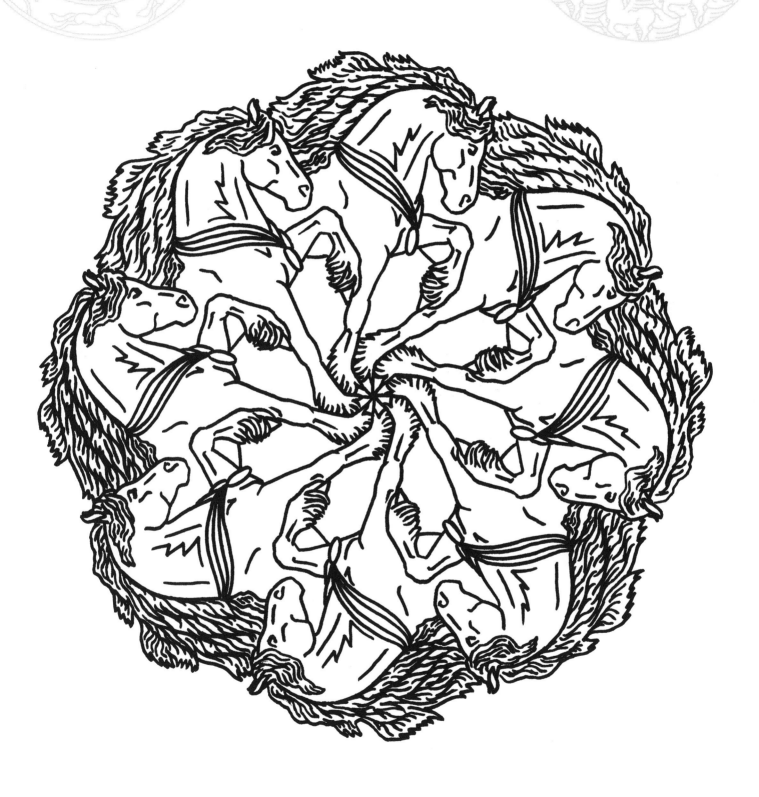

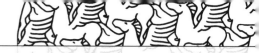

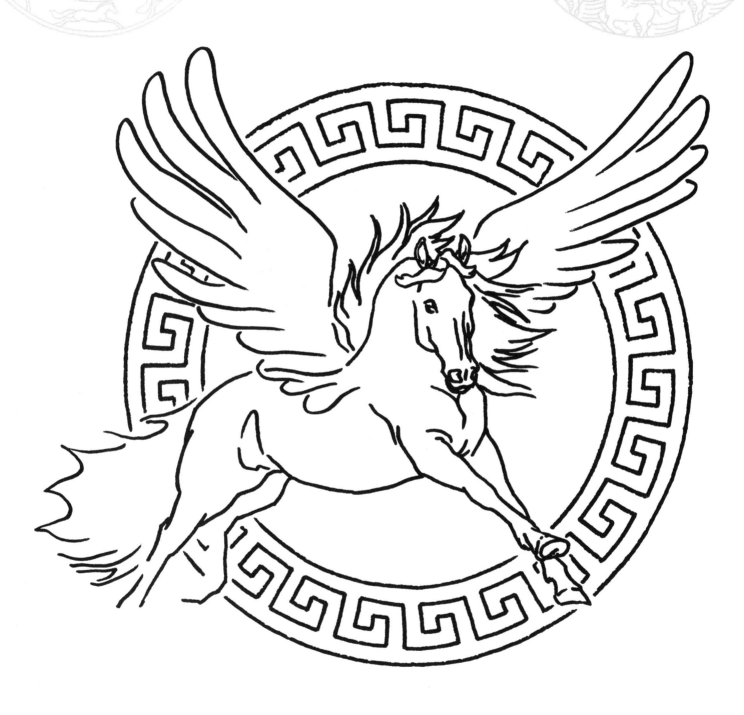

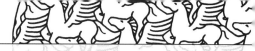

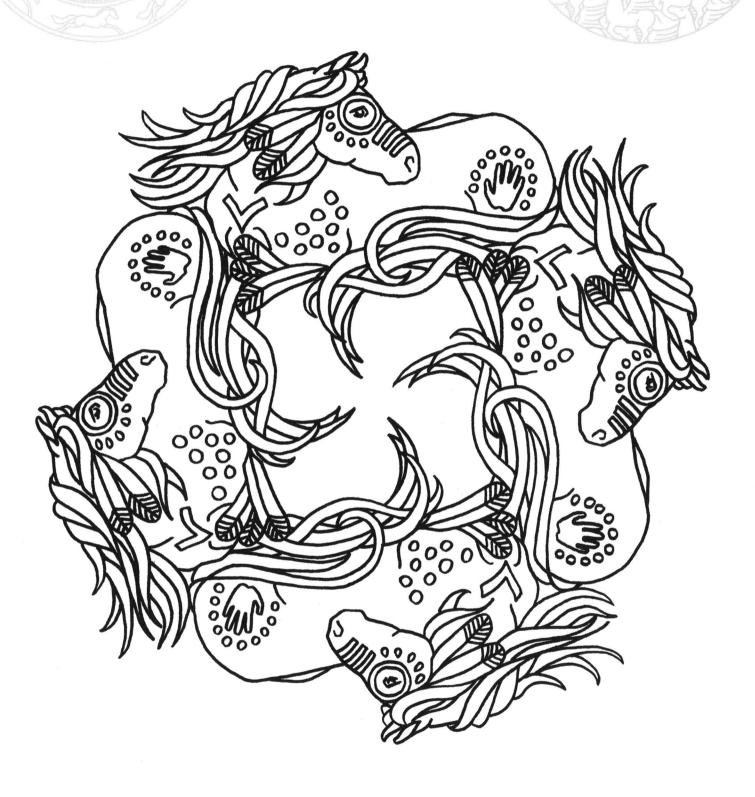

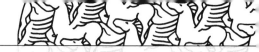

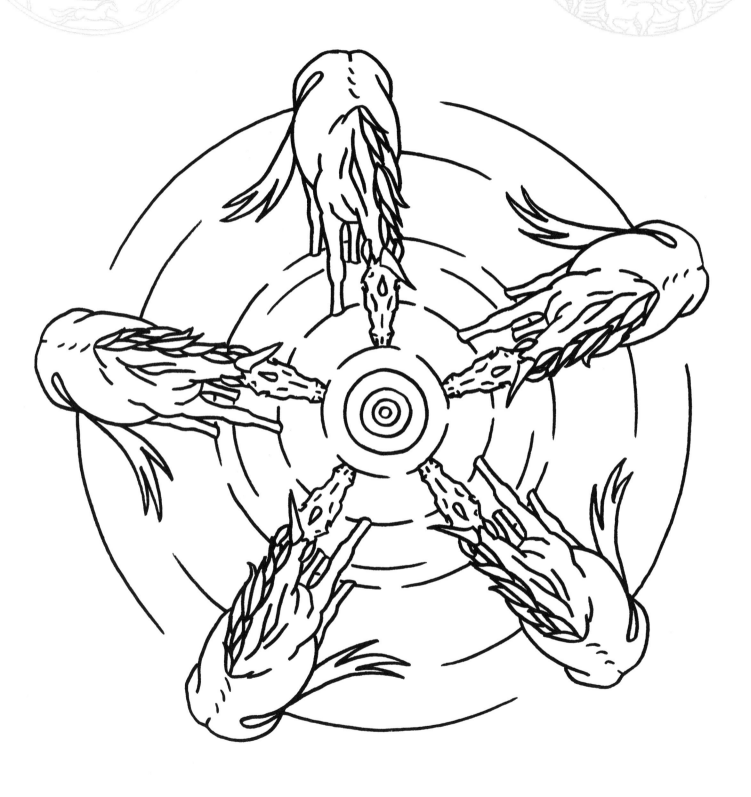

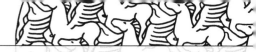

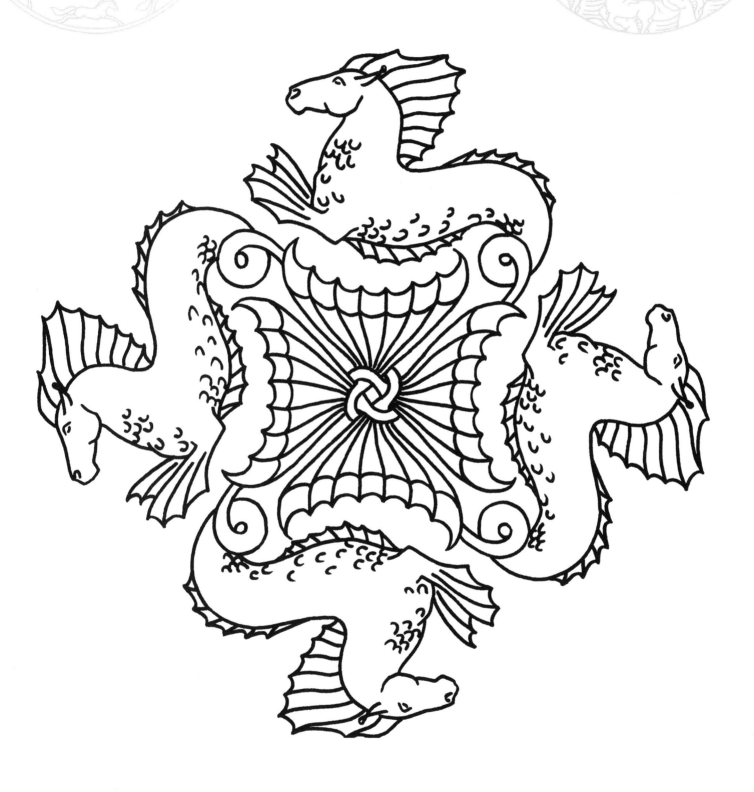

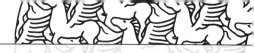

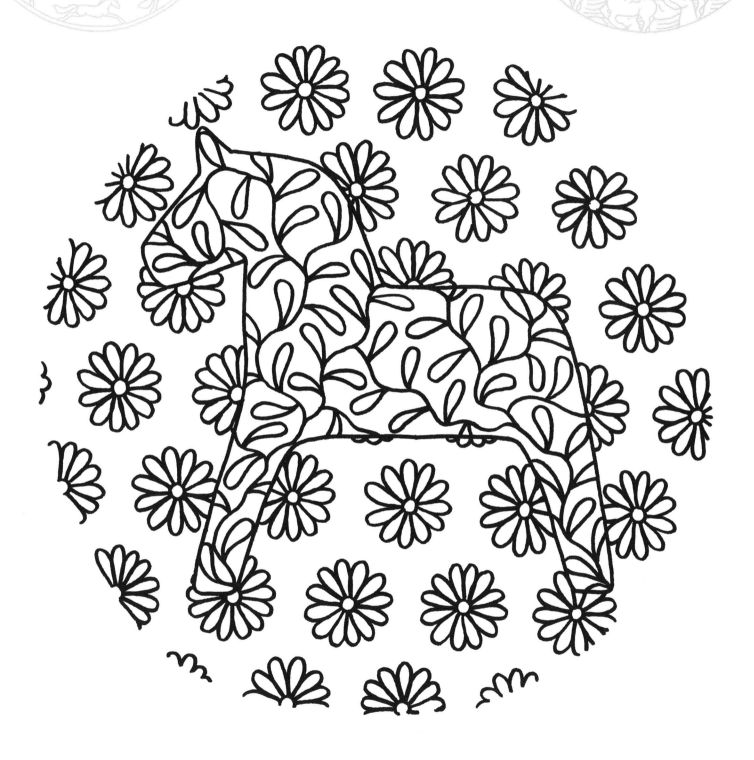

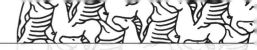

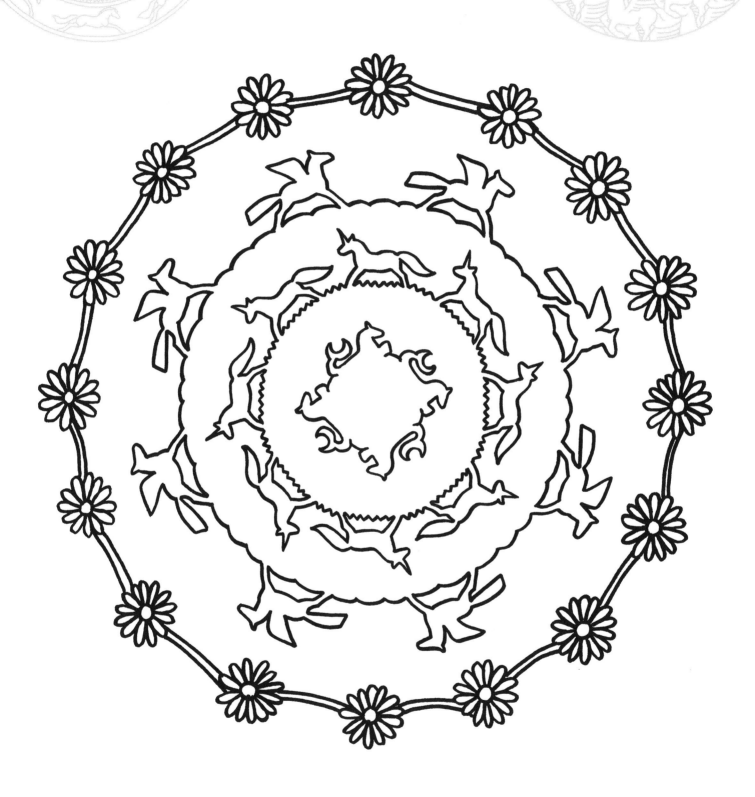

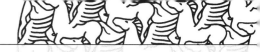

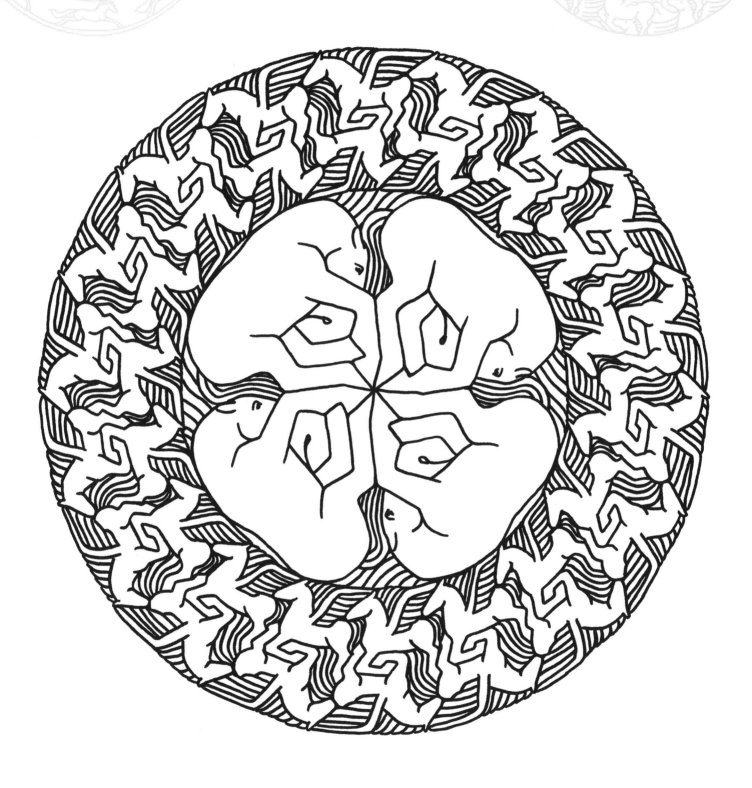

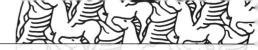

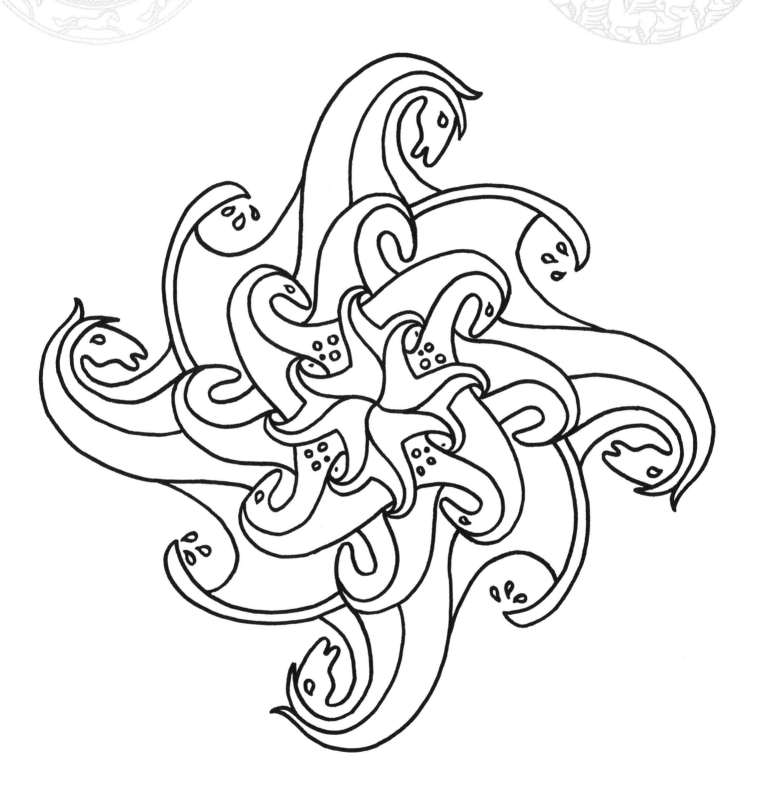

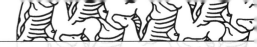

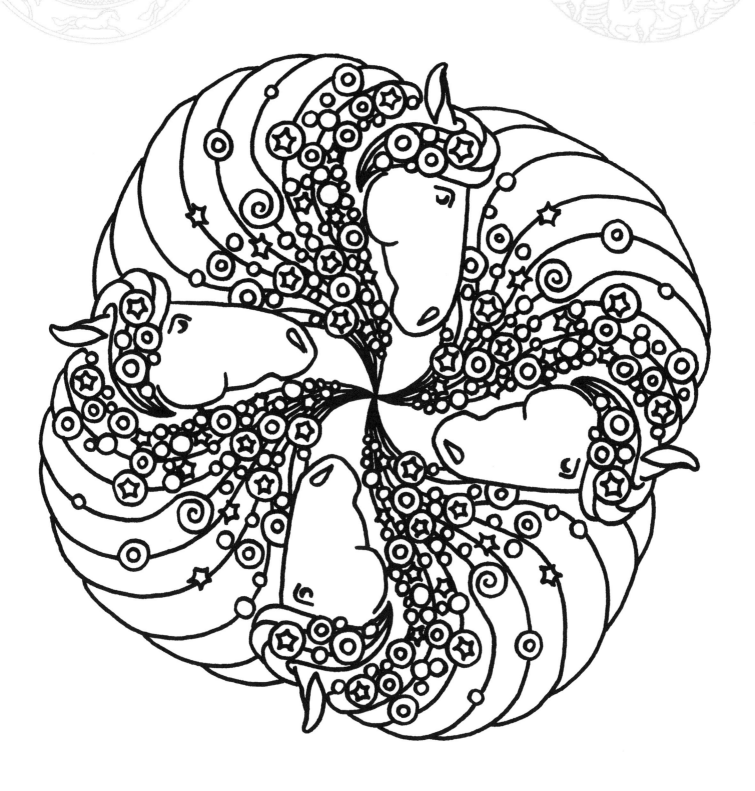

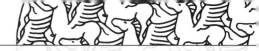

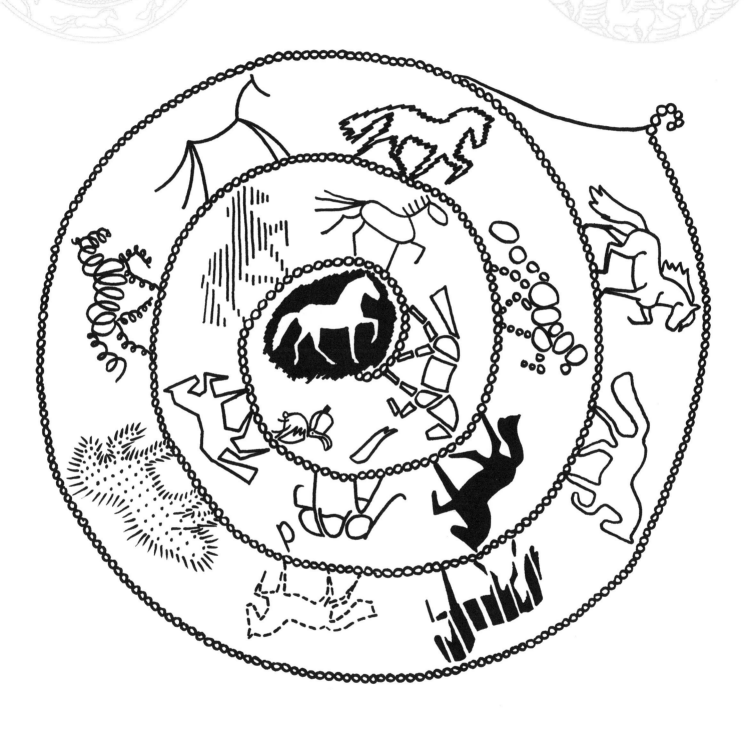

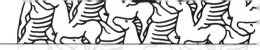

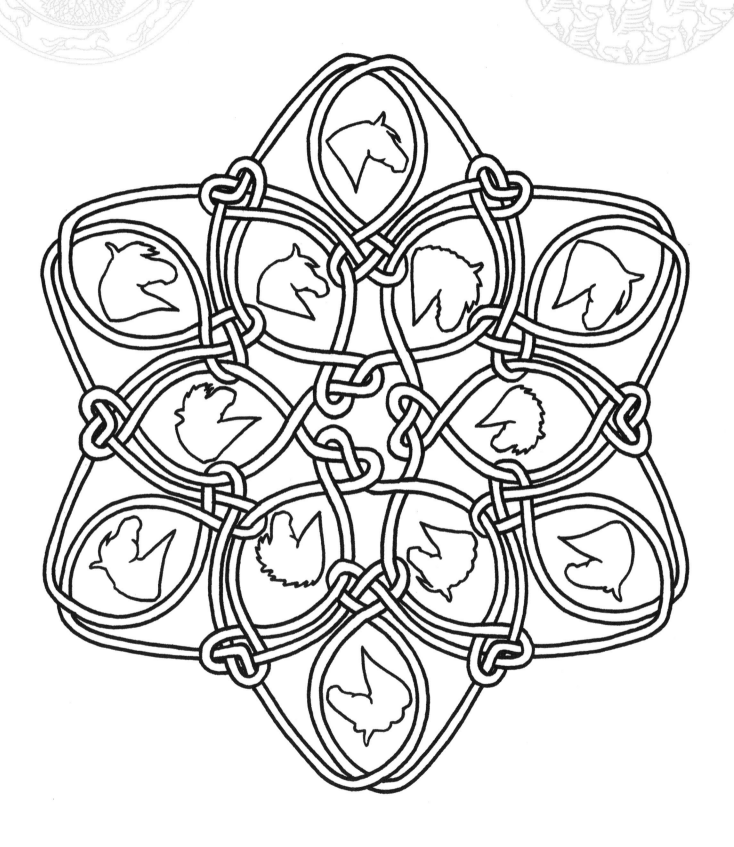

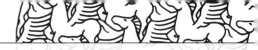

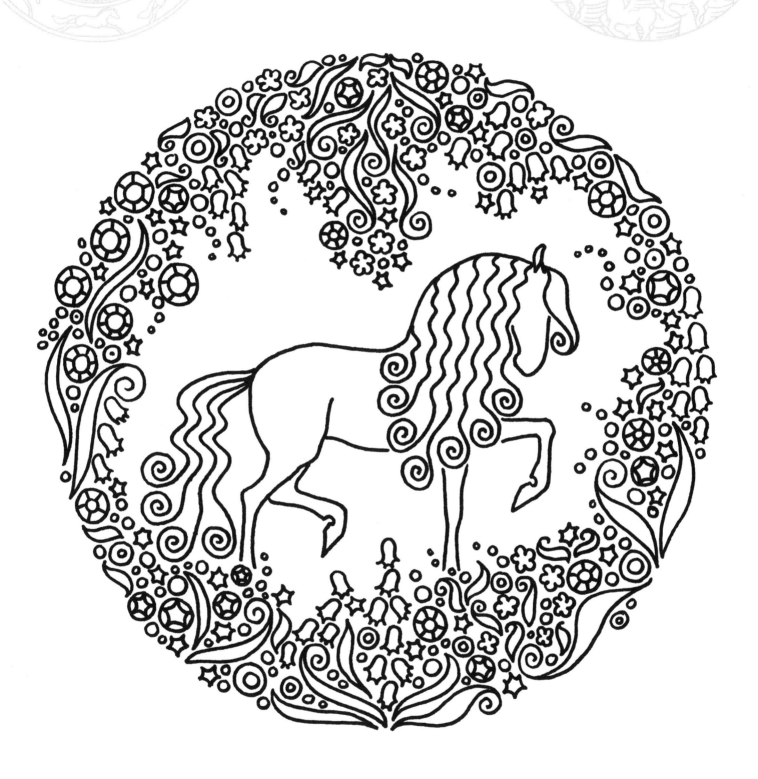

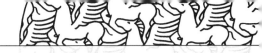

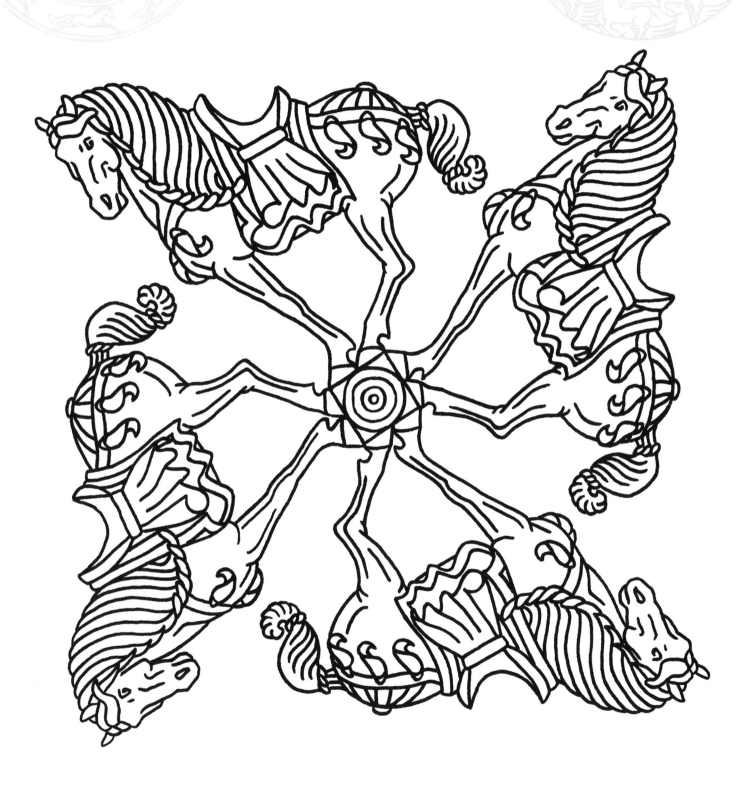

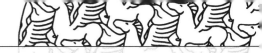

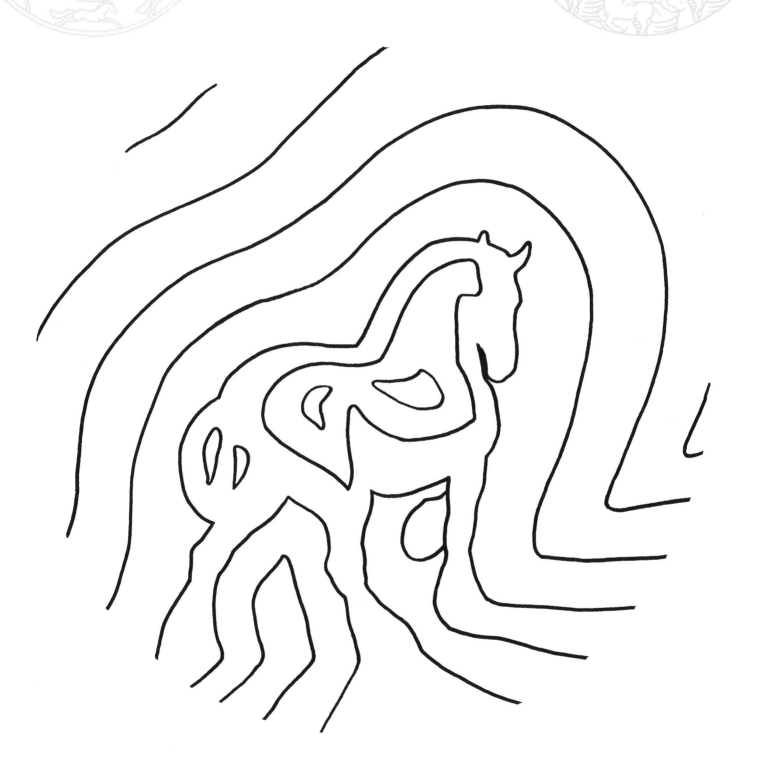

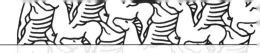

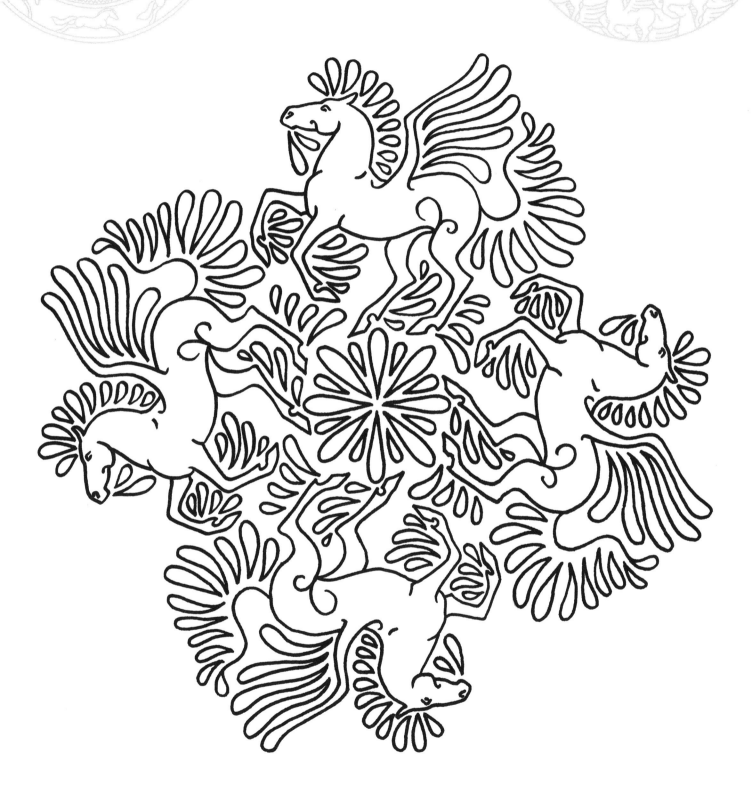

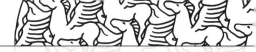

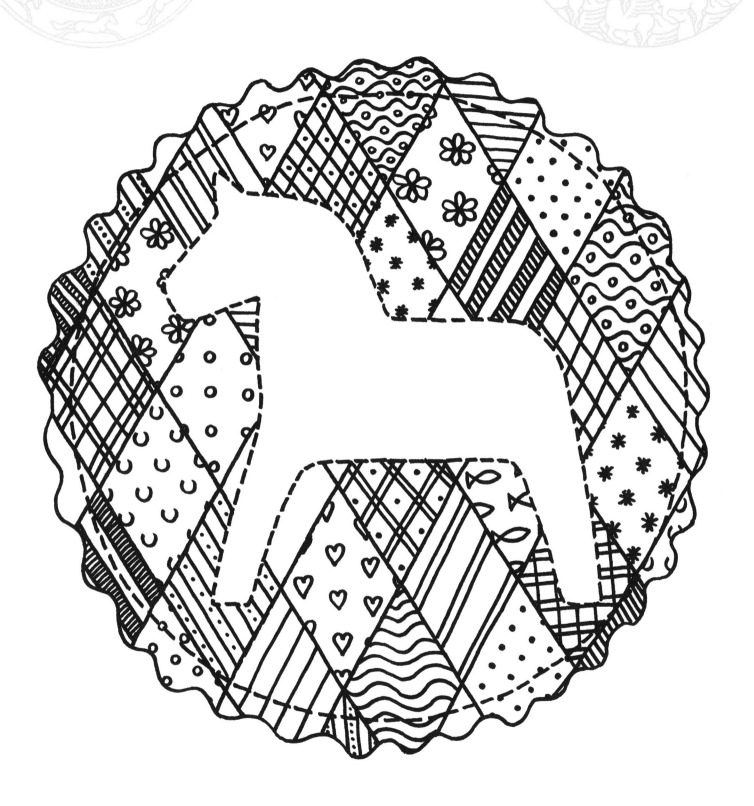

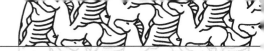

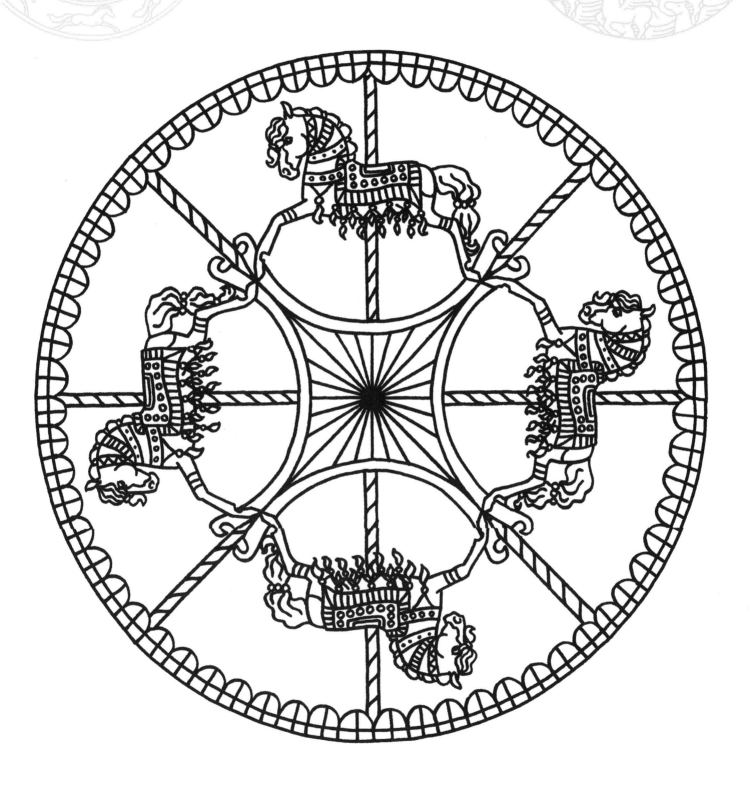

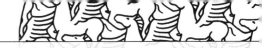

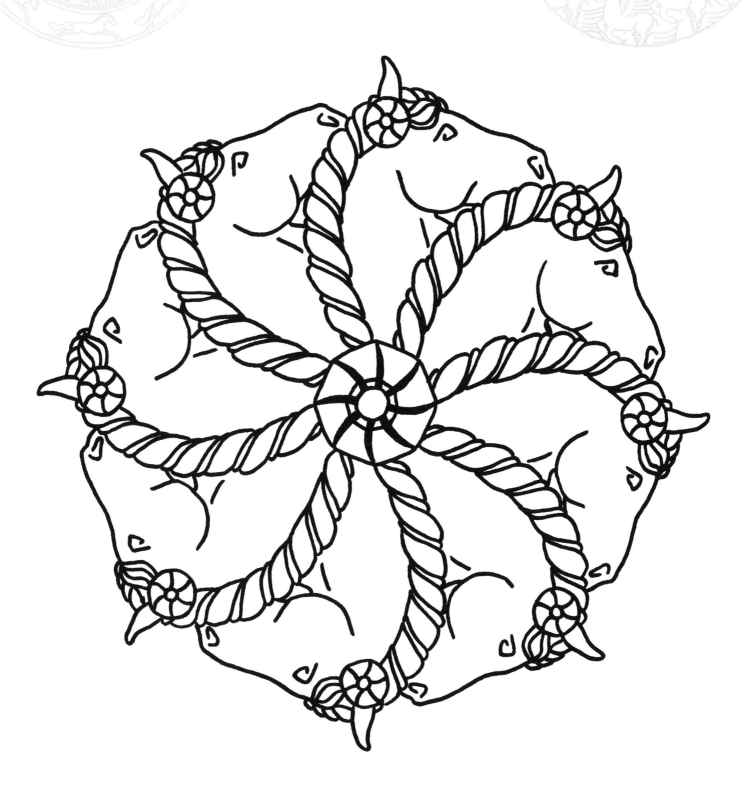

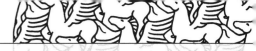

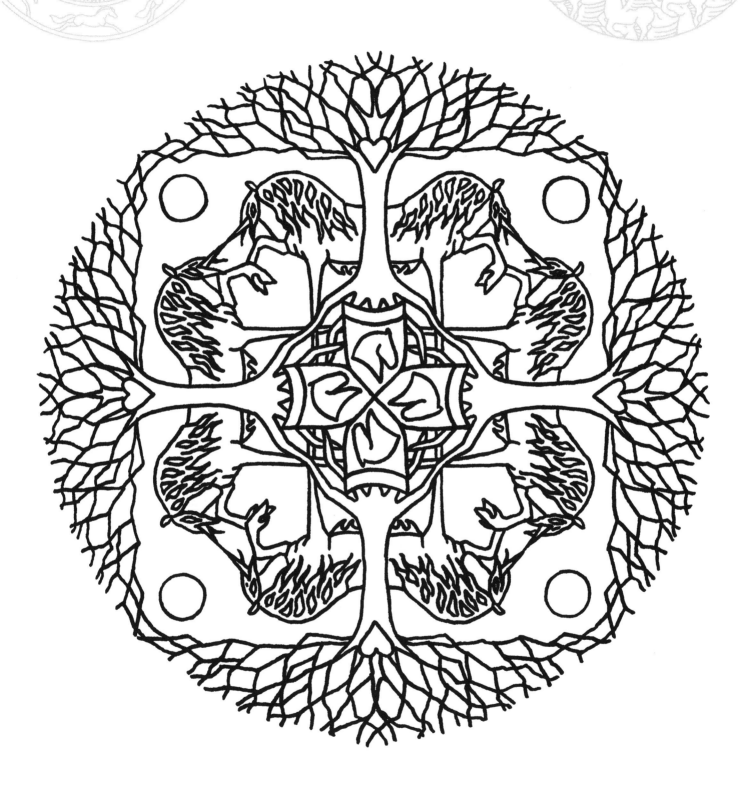

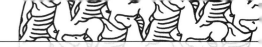

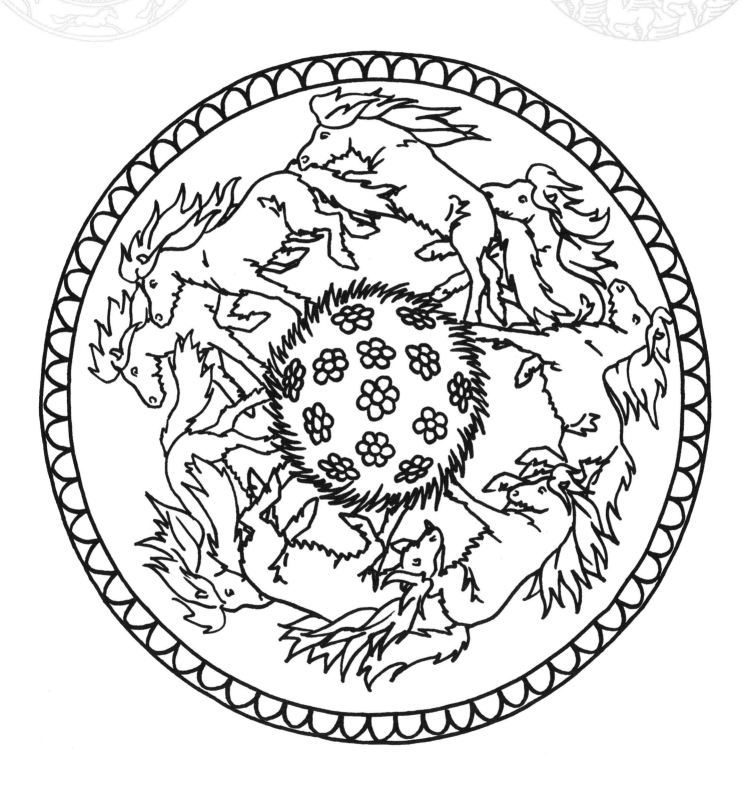

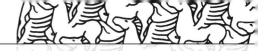
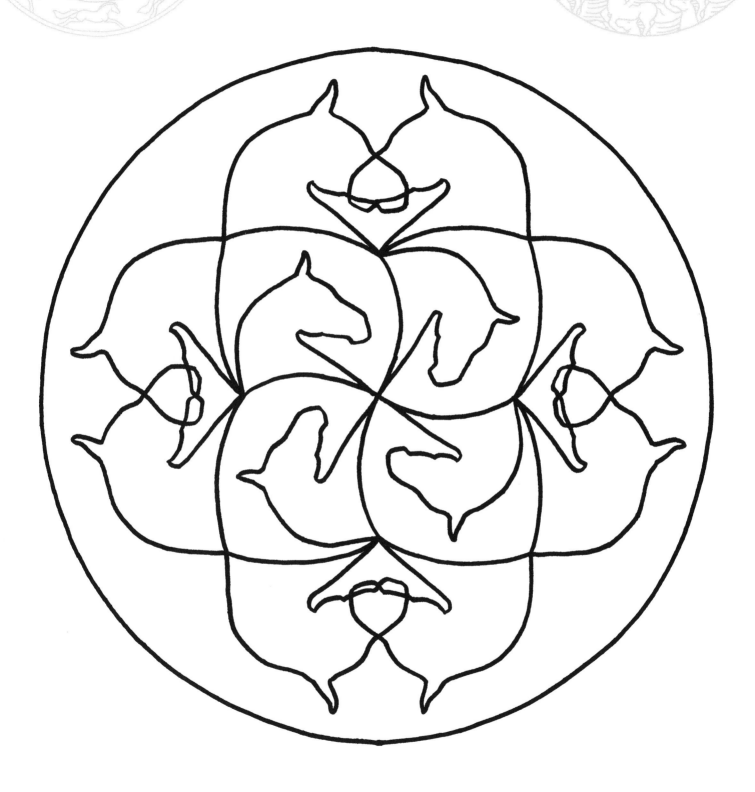

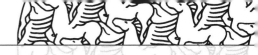

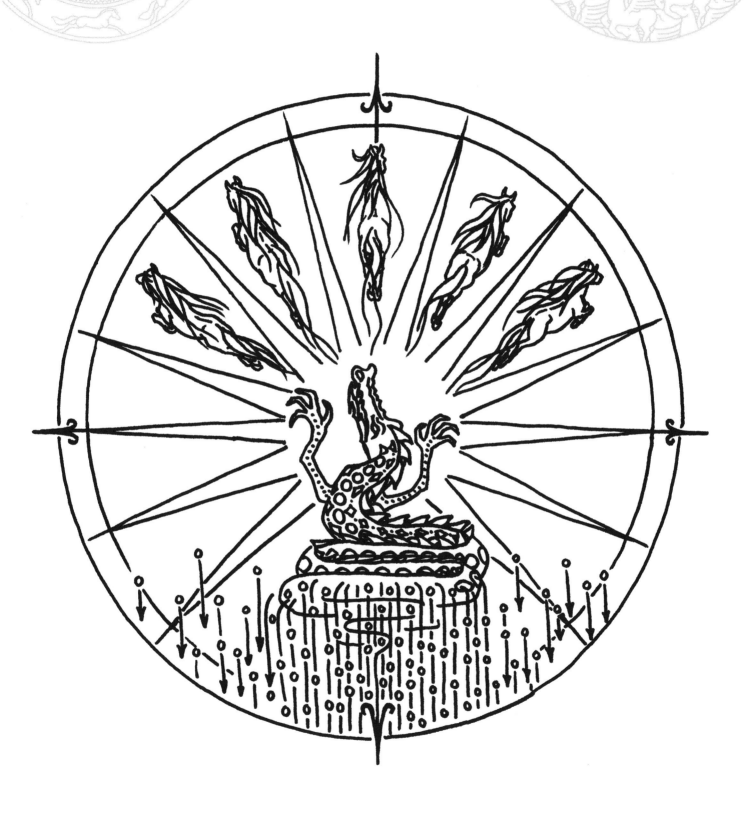

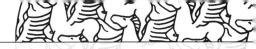

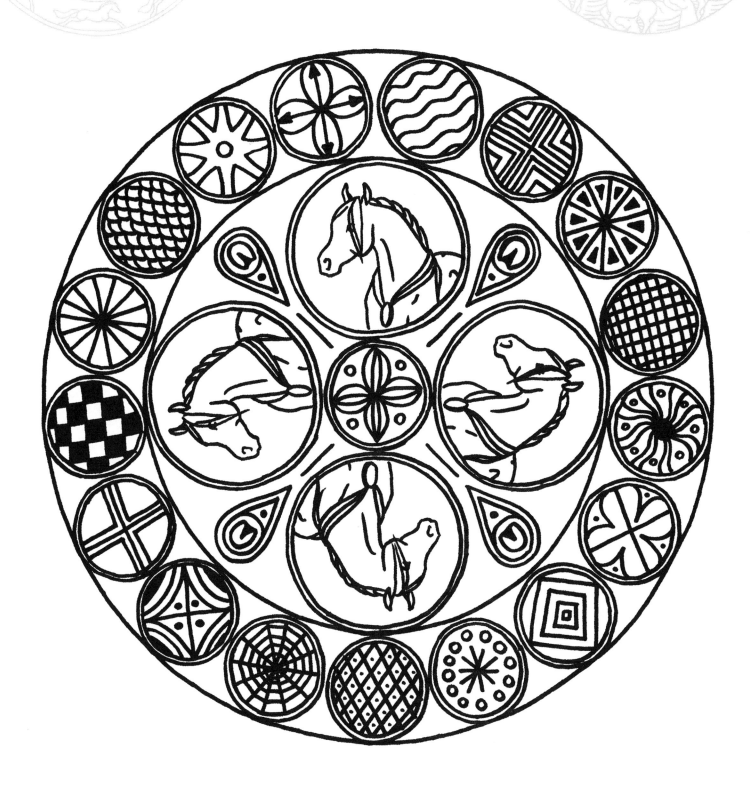

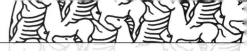

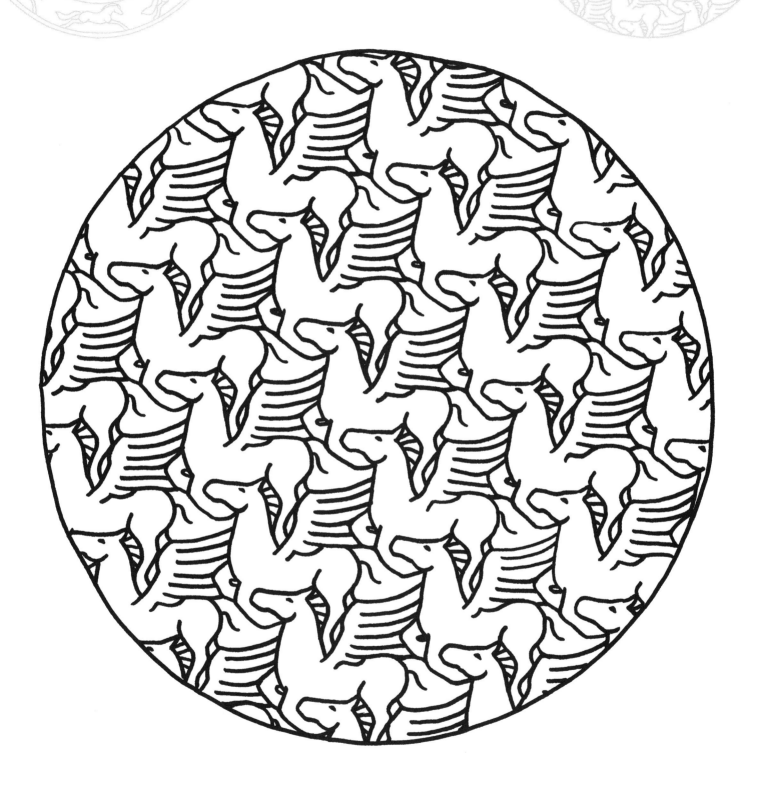

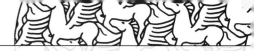

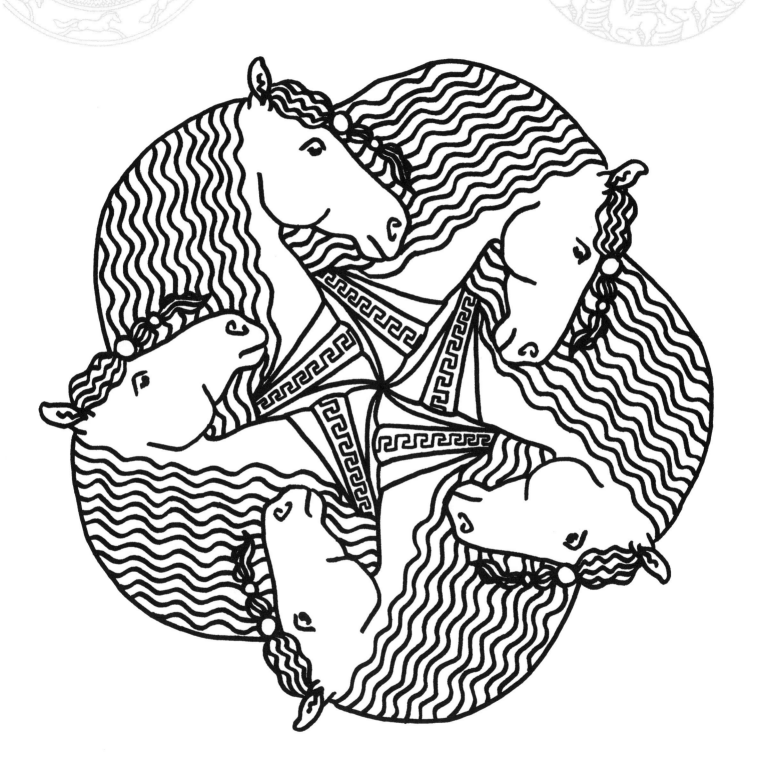

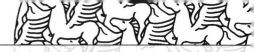

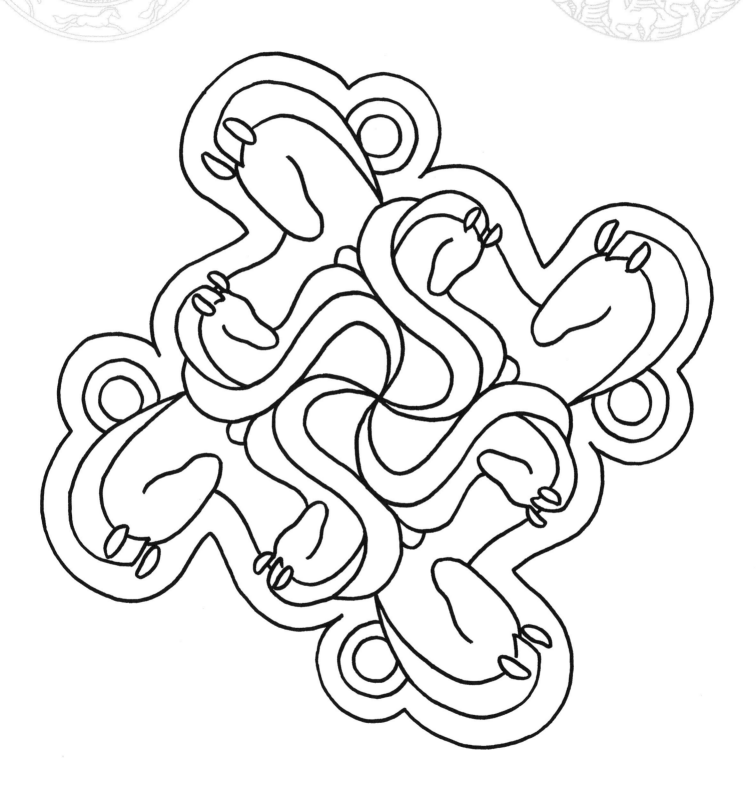

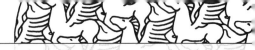

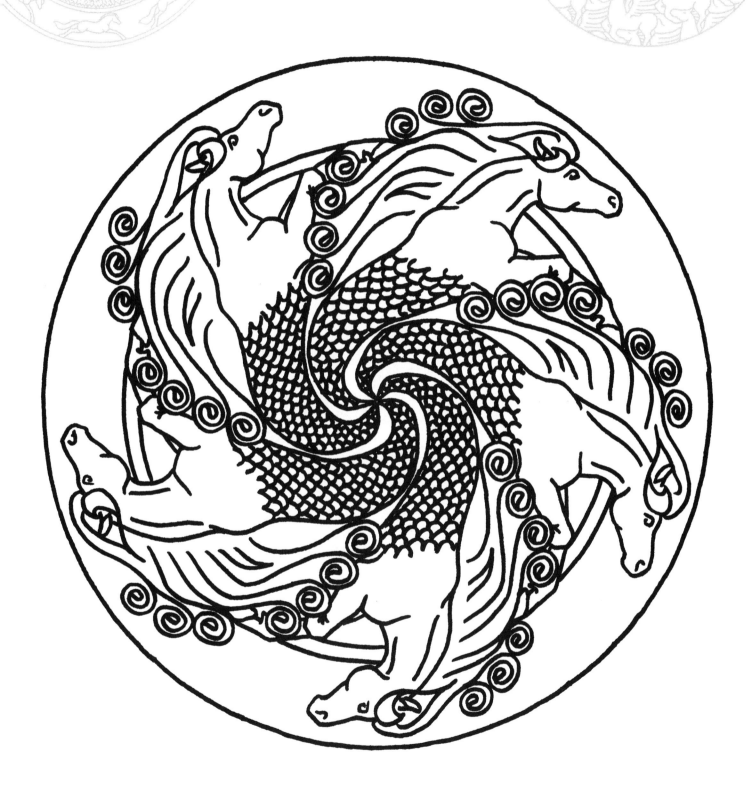

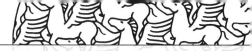

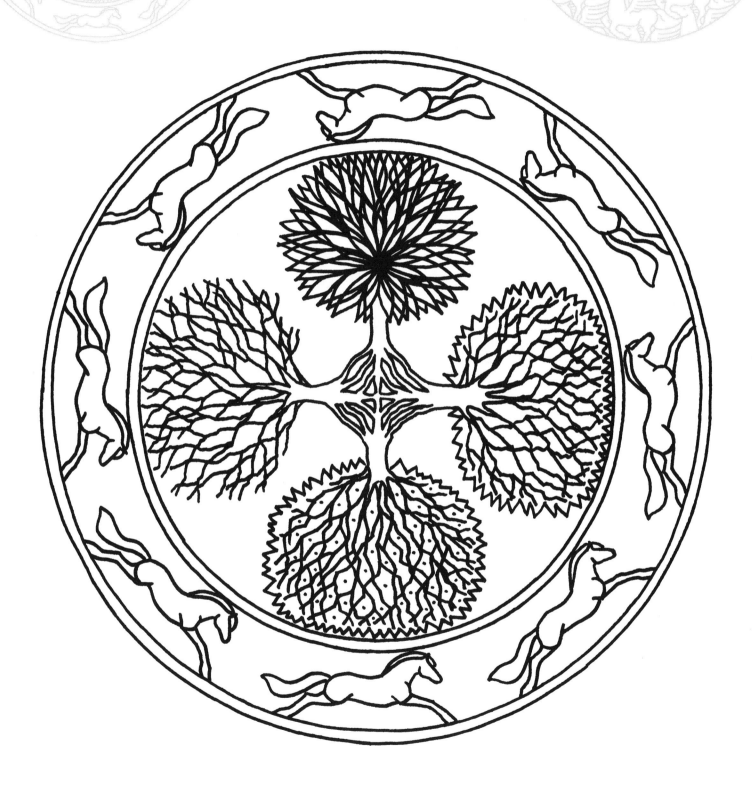

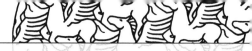

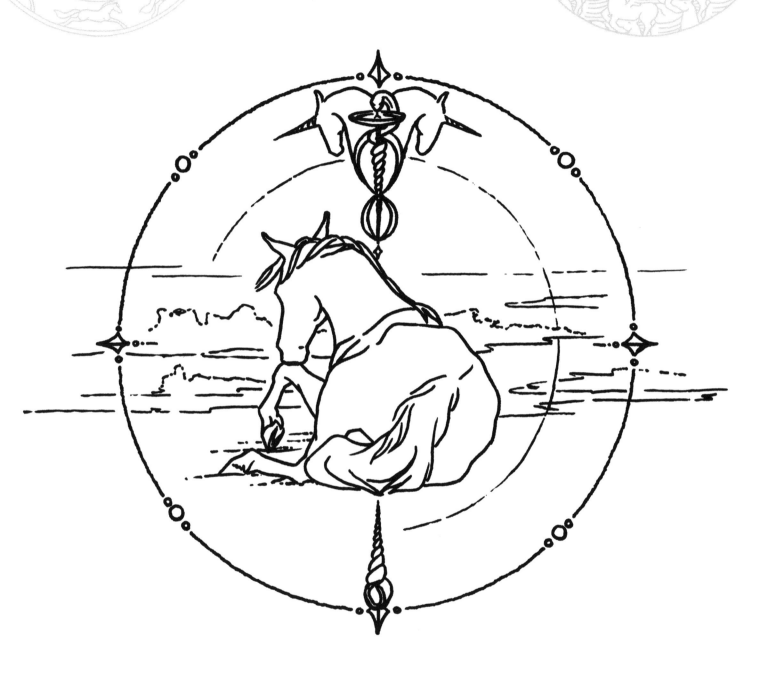

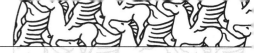

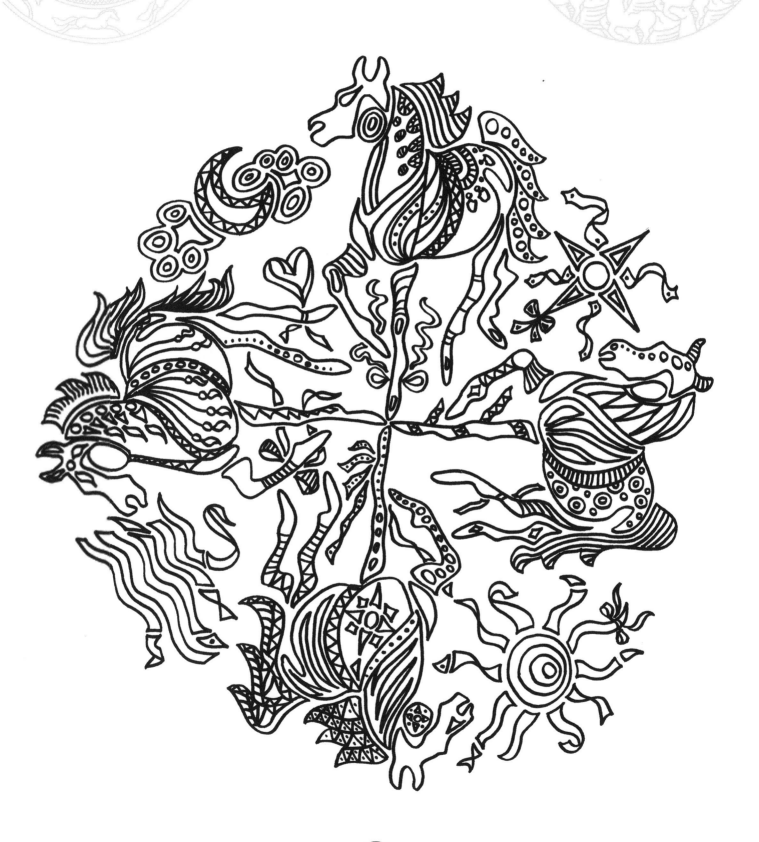

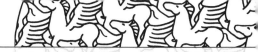

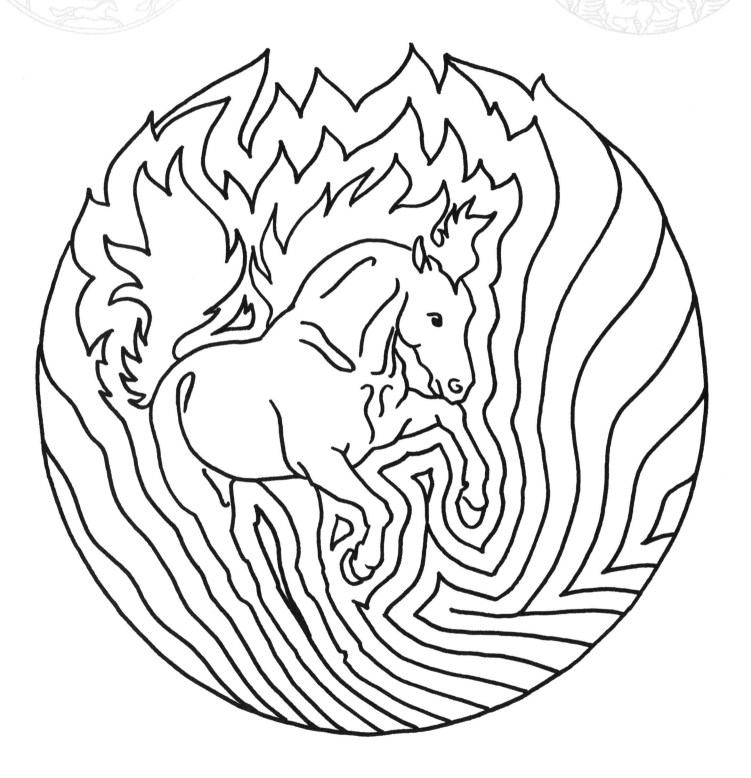

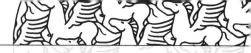

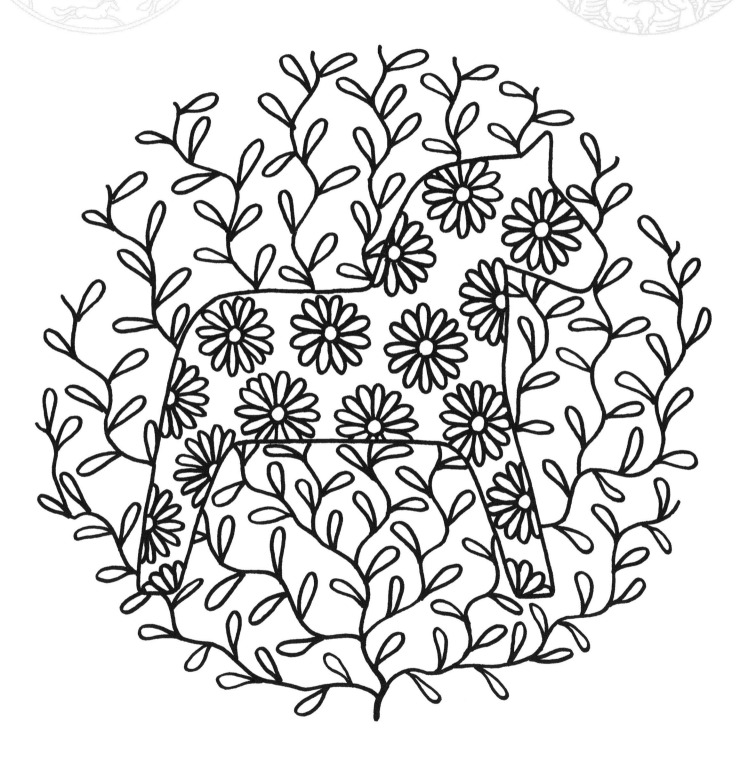

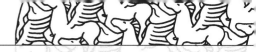

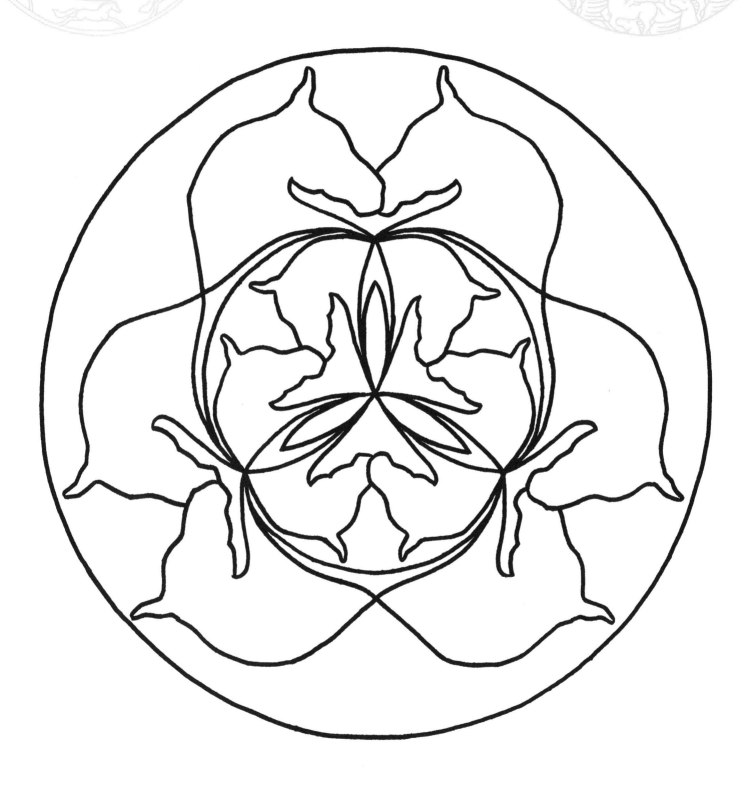

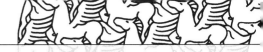

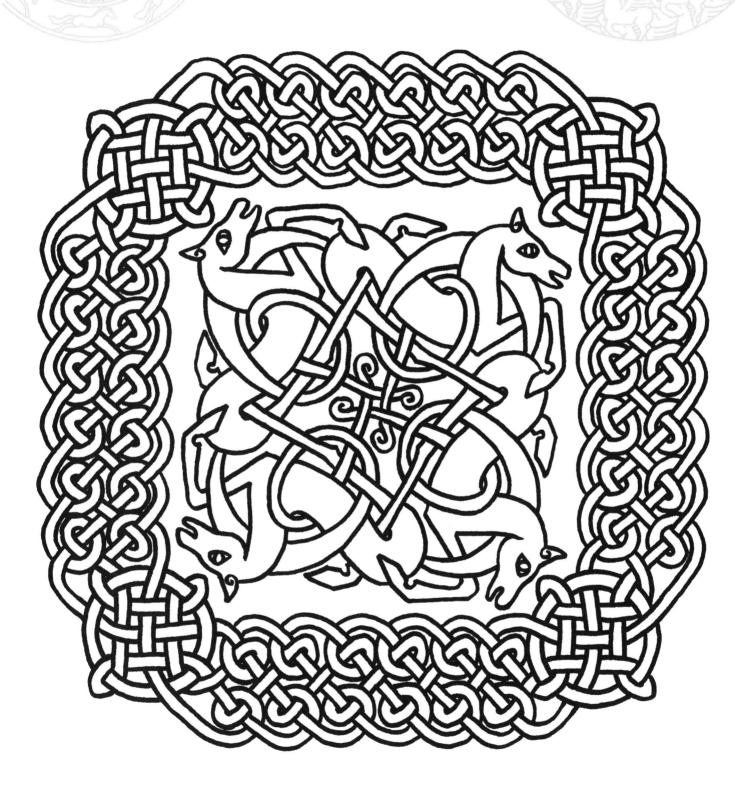

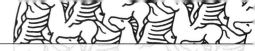

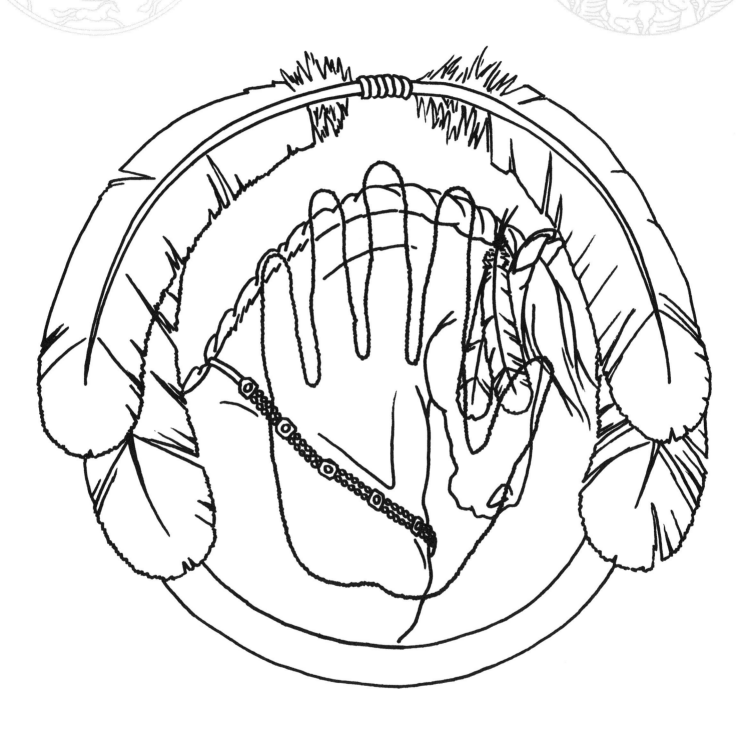

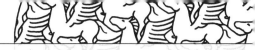

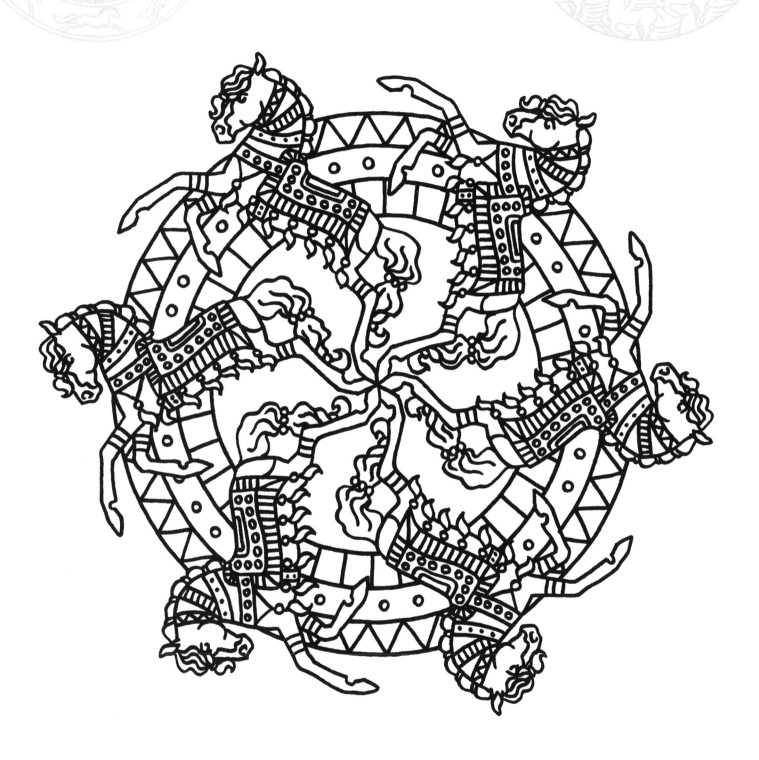

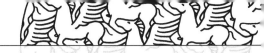

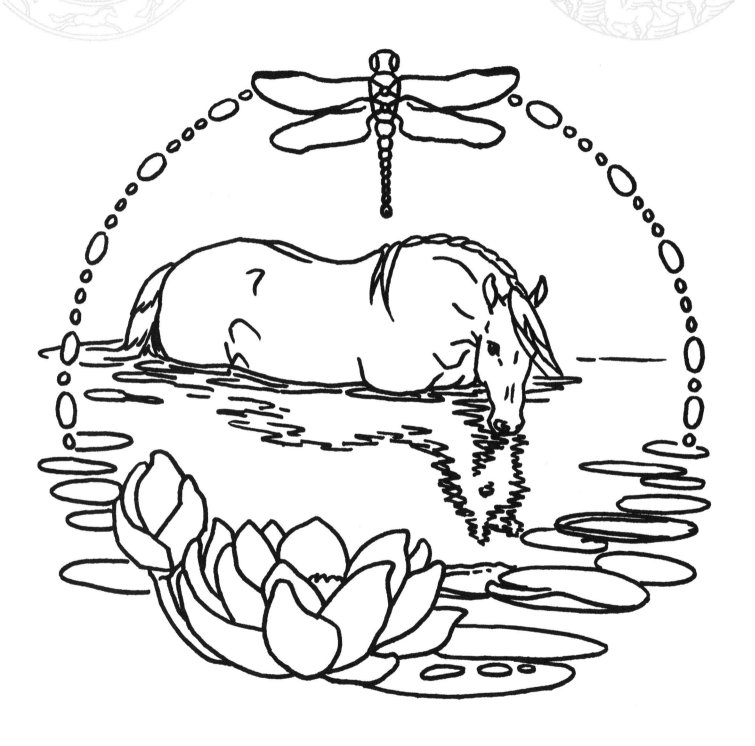

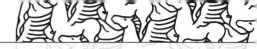

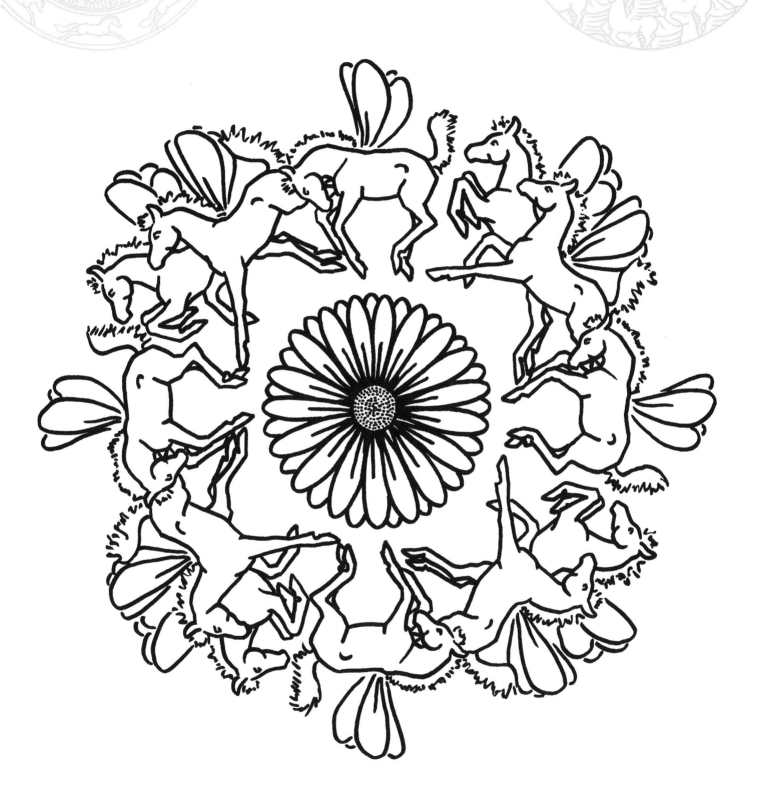

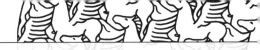

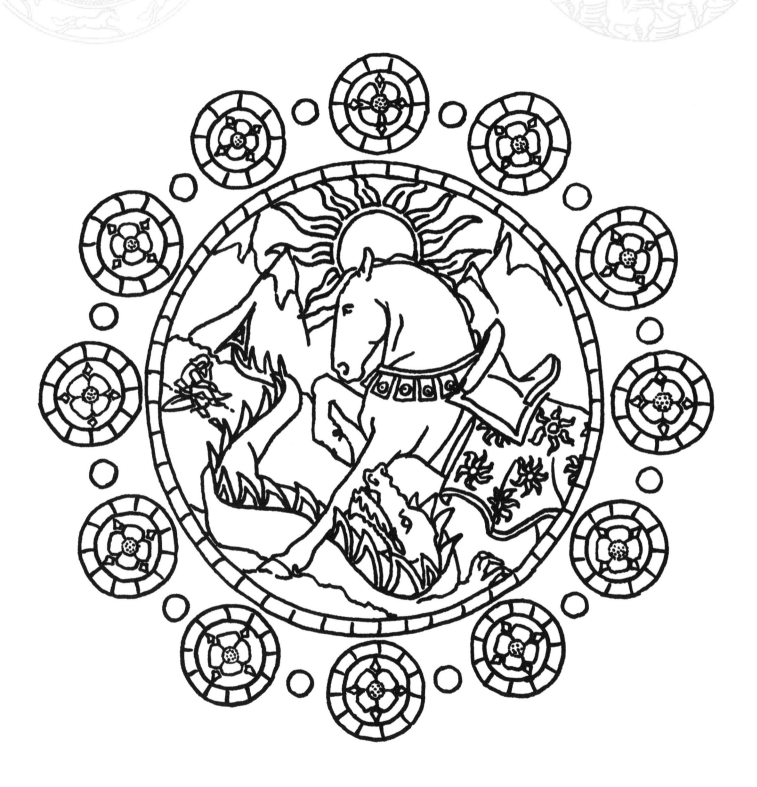

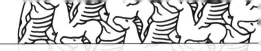

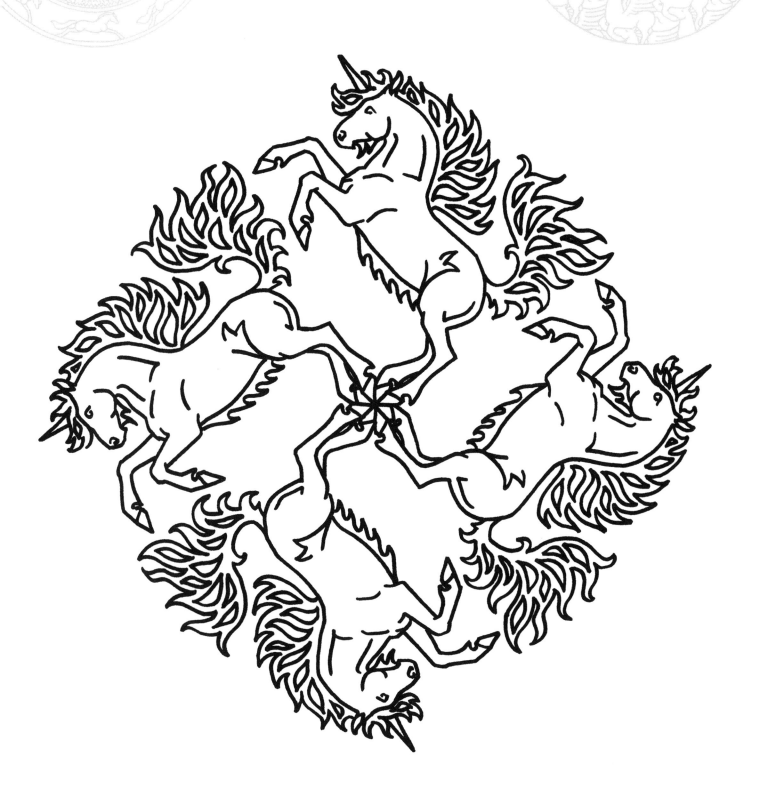

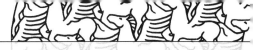

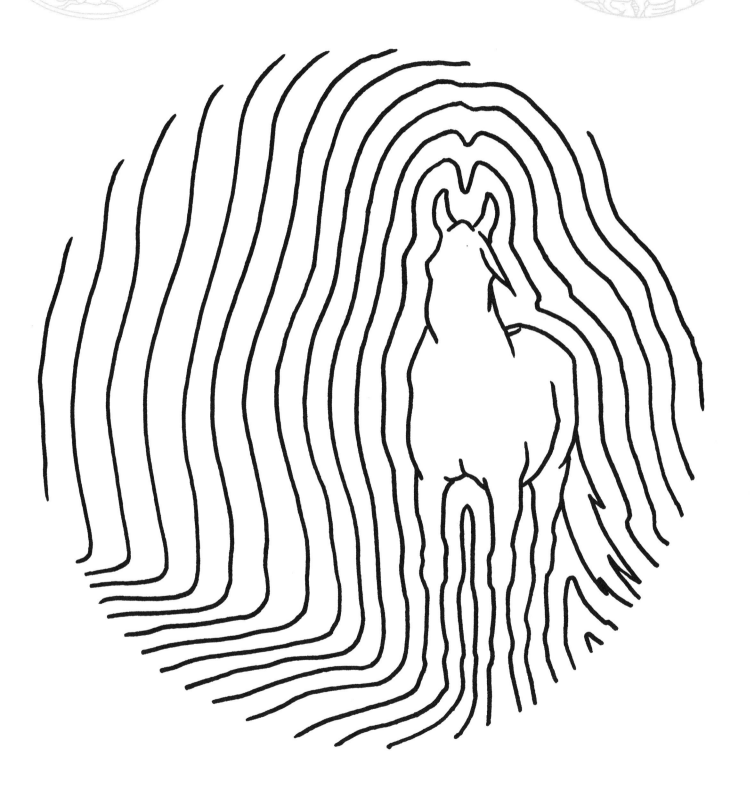

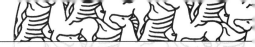

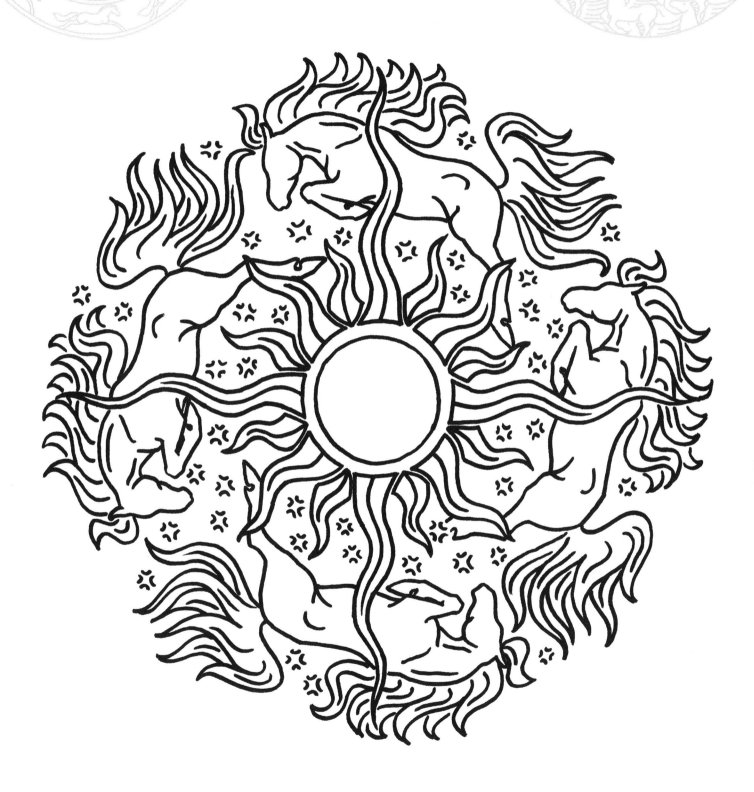

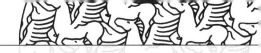

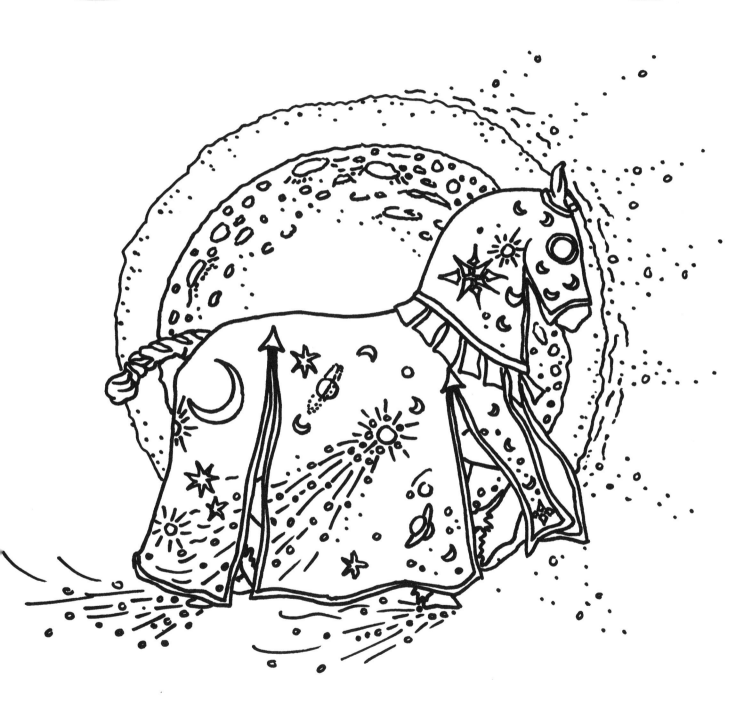

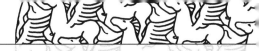

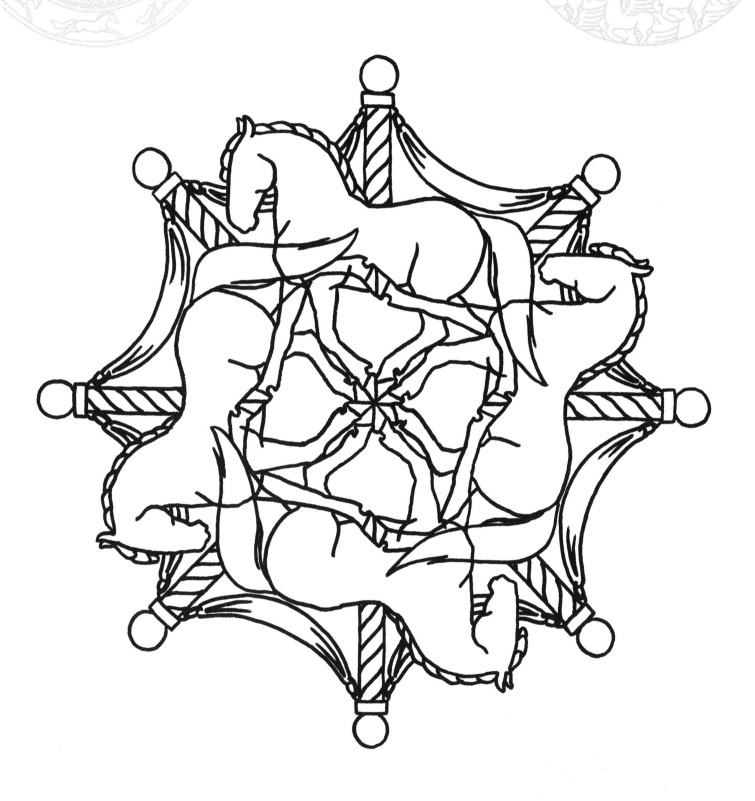

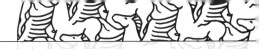

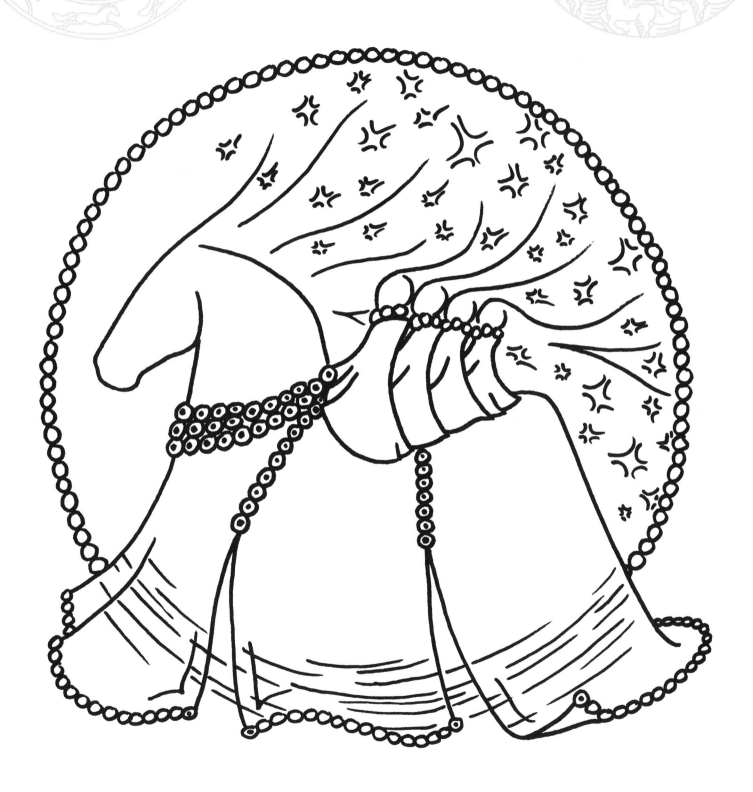

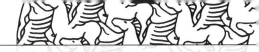

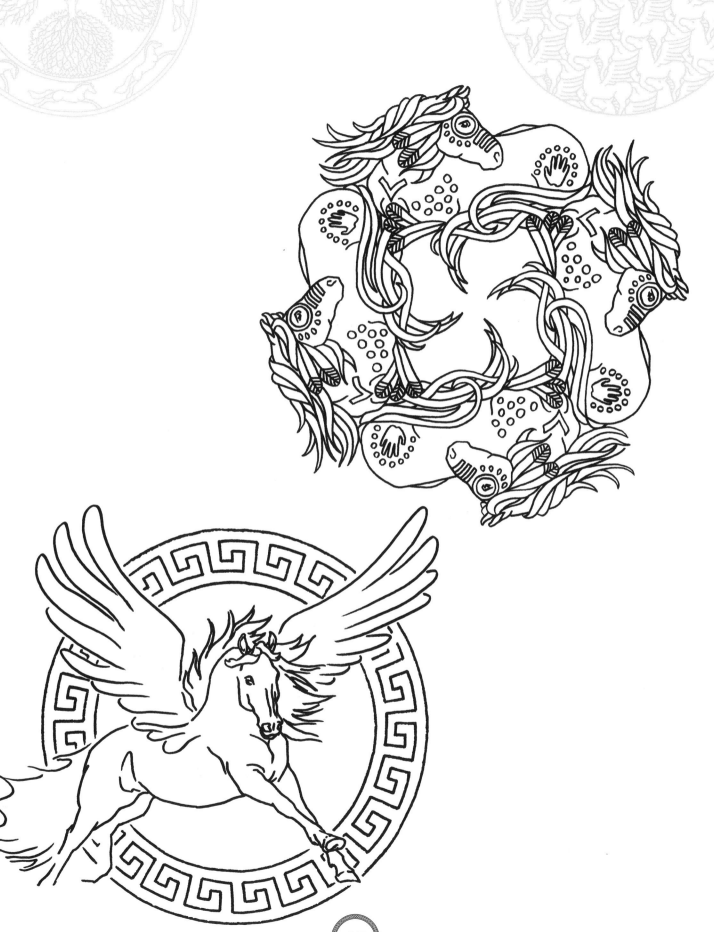

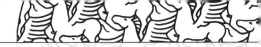

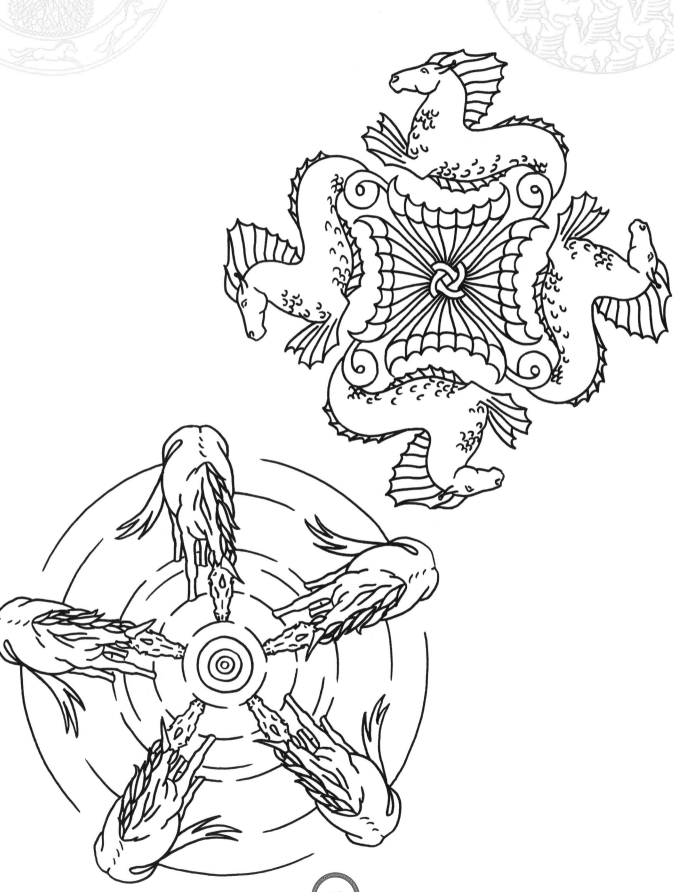

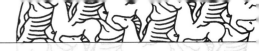

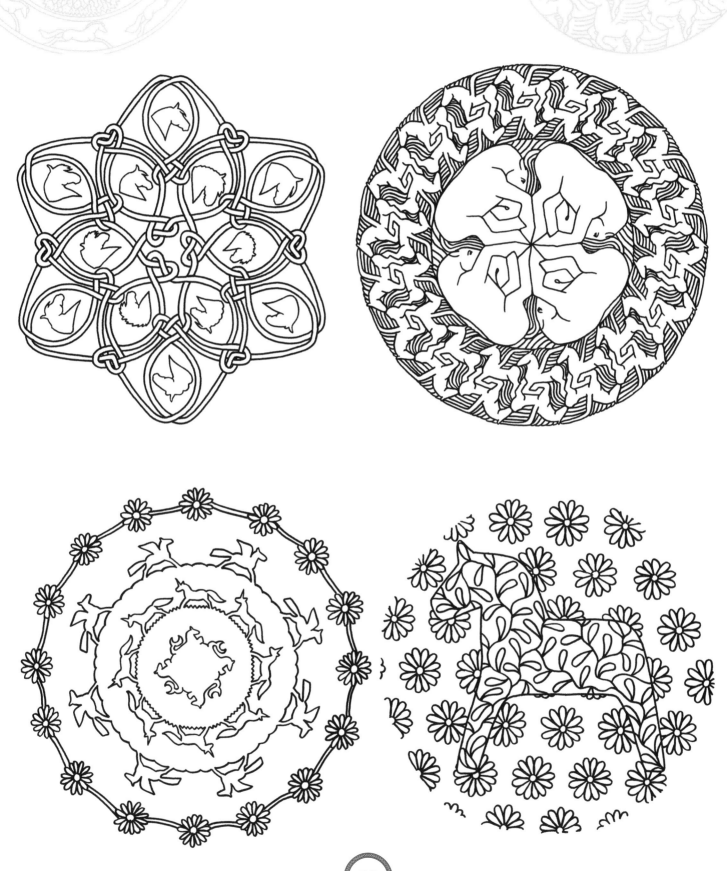

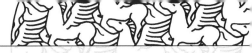

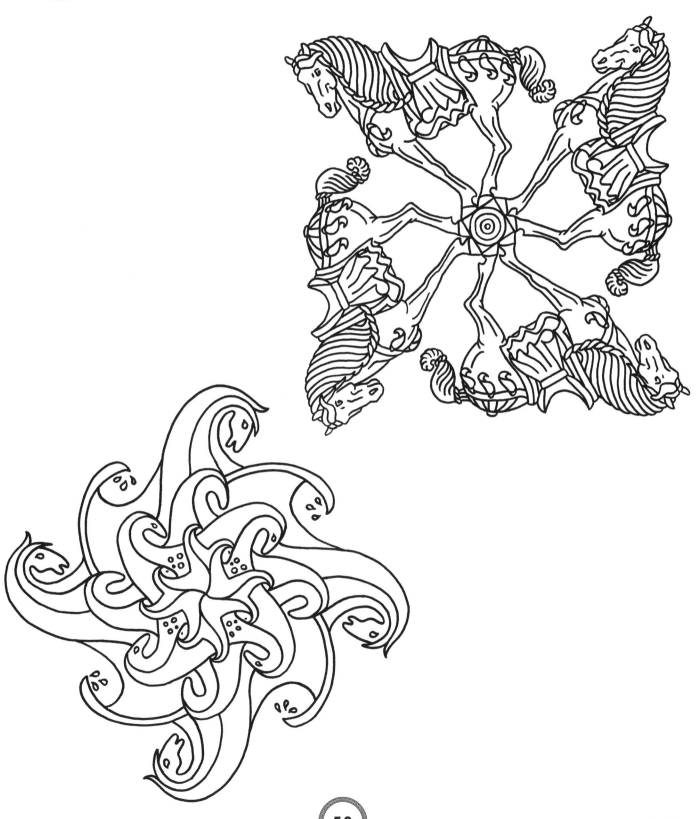

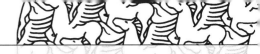

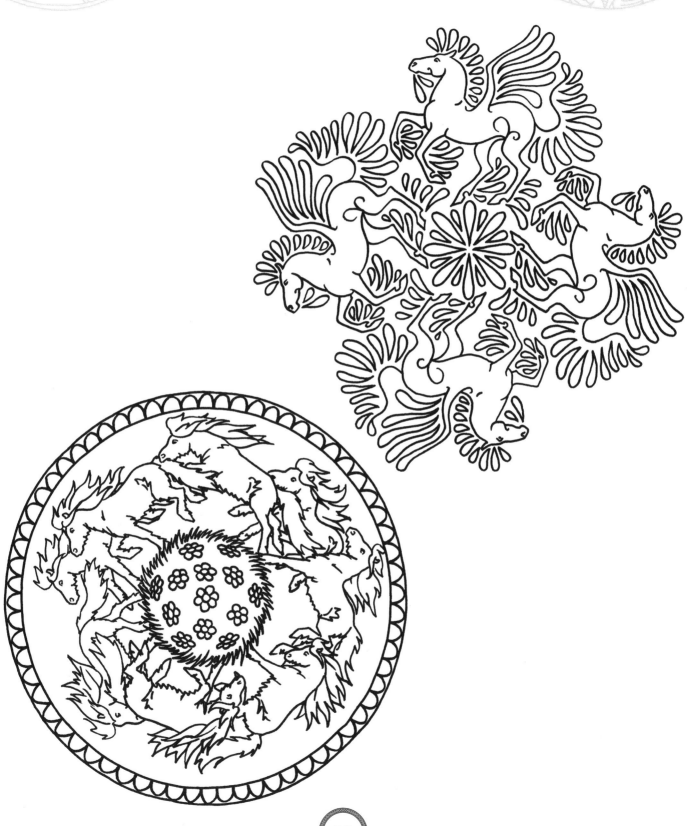

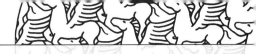

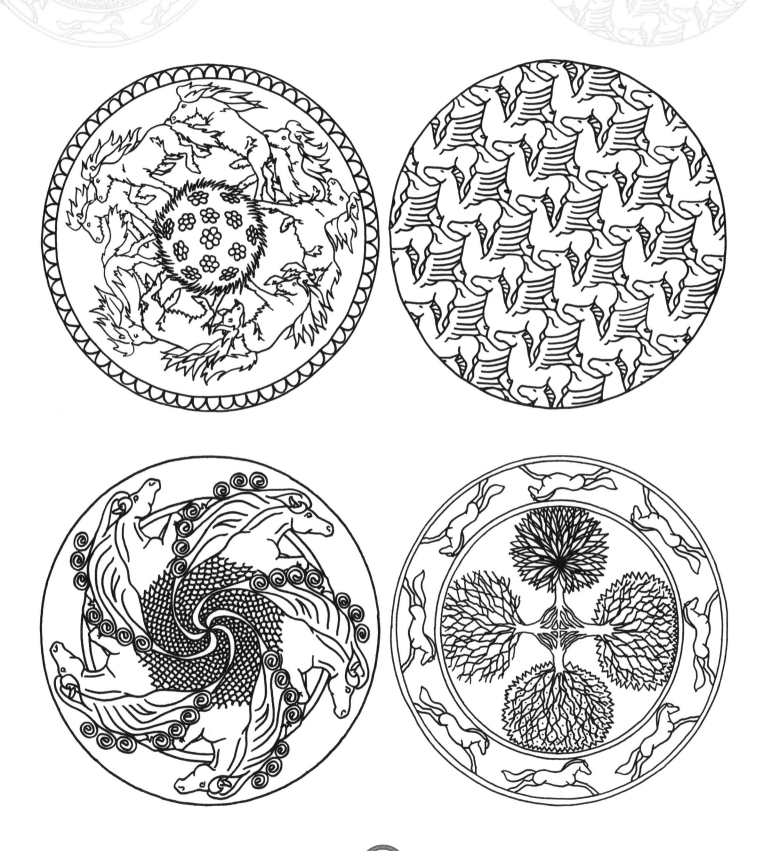

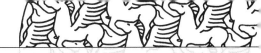

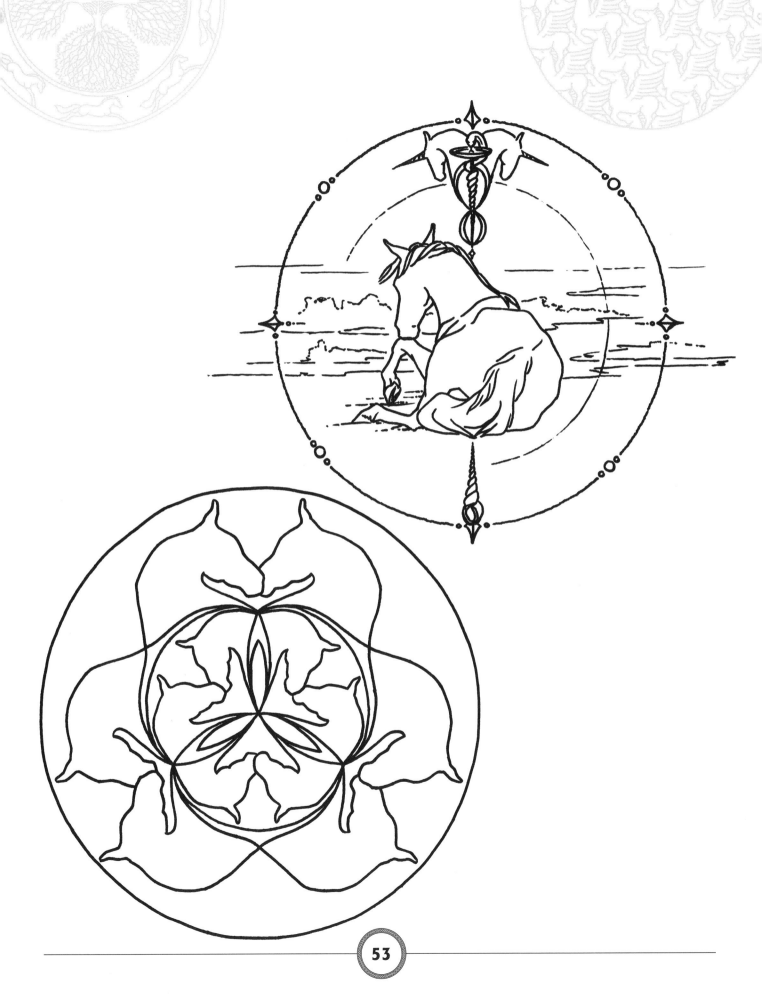

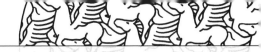

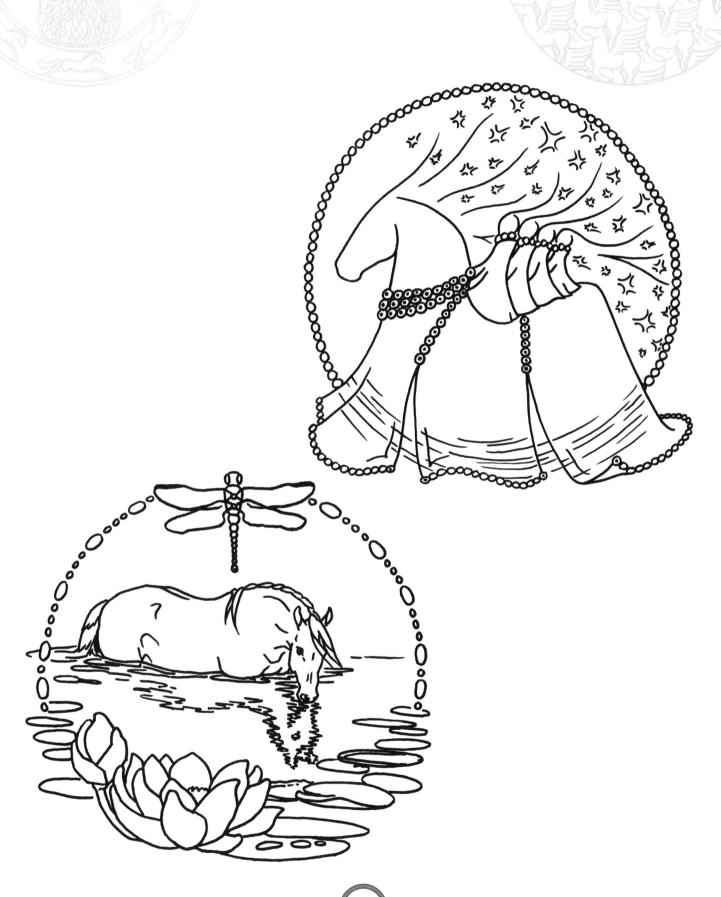